"With her signature poetic simplicity, Becca Stevens leads us bravely through her healing journey and along the path she has forged for so many wounded women—so that we can find our own way as both healed and healer. Reading this book is like being anointed with the very oils she writes about."

—Nancy Rue, Christy Award–winning author of The Reluctant Prophet trilogy, inspired by Magdalene and Thistle Farms

"This book is a fascinating life story of a woman who took the evil done to her and used it for the motivation to do good for abused women around the world. She has been God's instrument for healing and hope for countless numbers of broken women across America."

—Tony Campolo, Ph.D., Eastern University

"Only Becca Stevens can write a book extolling the virtues of being a snake oil salesman and have us believe it. After reading this, I'm ready to be anointed!"

—Marshall Chapman, author of *They Came to Nashville* and *Goodbye, Little Rock and Roller*

"Some old-timey snake oil salesmen offered the Gospel and then sold their products. Becca Stevens does it the other way around. This book helps explain why her way works better."

—Don Schlitz, Grammy Award–winning songwriter

"Becca Stevens is a spiritual alchemist of the highest order, mediating eternal healing through an elixir of truth-telling, compassionate regard, relentless hope, and indefatigable spirit. Within this modest volume resides the recipe for authentic love and the promise of life renewed. She is a treasure, and more, she is a mentor/leader for our time concerning the things that matter most of all."
—Stephen Bauman, author of *Simple Truths: On Values, Civility and Our Common Good*

"Becca is a fearless warrior for those in need of hope and healing; her words speak to the power of unconditional love. We are so grateful for Becca, and the unwavering vision she shares with all of us."   —John and Fiona Prine

Snake Oil

The Art of Healing
and Truth-Telling

BECCA STEVENS

Peace & love
Becca Stevens

JERICHO
BOOKS

New York • Boston • Nashville

The author is represented by Creative Trust, Inc.

Jericho Books
Hachette Book Group
237 Park Avenue
New York, NY 10017
www.jerichobooks.com.

Printed in the United States of America

First Edition: March 2013
10 9 8 7 6 5 4 3 2

RRD-C

Jericho Books is an imprint of Hachette Book Group, Inc.

The Jericho Books name and logo are trademarks of Hachette Book Group, Inc.

The Hachette Speakers Bureau provides a wide range of authors for speaking events. To find out more, go to www.HachetteSpeakersBureau.com or call (866) 376-6591.

The publisher is not responsible for websites (or their content) that are not owned by the publisher.

Library of Congress Control Number : 2013930183

In many ways this is *The Story of How I Learned That Making Oils Helps Heal the World*. That never would have been possible without the original board of Magdalene, and it is to this group and the first volunteers and residents that I dedicate this book—especially Gilbert, Dick, Cary, Charlie, Alice, Jane, Jeff, Linda, Julia, Carole, Tori, Bobby, Rick, Michael, Rod, Regina, Marlei, Vali, Cheryl, Sandy, Angie, Kay, Sigourney, Carlana, Stephanie, Mark, Tim, Stacy, Levi, Marcus, Jill, Toni, Holli, Marshall, and Matraca. You gave life to a dream of sanctuary.

KUDZU MADONNA

A Kudzu Madonna on the side of a highway
Calls to searching pilgrims in need of a sign.
Draped in the abundance of earth,
She is a vision holding out her healing hand.
Her forgiving nature is our first healer
As she dispenses her gifts like grace.
Her flowers, trees, and hidden treasures
Are offerings from her sacred heart.
There are mysteries in the weeds
That make the world a mystical place.
There is truth in the grass and clover
That covers the whole earth with a healing balm.

—BECCA STEVENS

Contents

Contents

Foreword

Who hasn't been down at the crossroads, wondering if you'll find your way home? Becca Stevens, a "snake oil" purveyor, has. I met her in Nashville, along with her extraordinary people, the women of Magdalene who had lived lives of prostitution and drug addiction. These women, who were of all ethnicities, believed that making oil from crushed herbs, bottling the glistening liquid, and then wrapping the boxes in rough paper "made of thistle" was a metaphor for their lives.

"We'd growed up all ugly and tough, and nobody could tell us nothing. And now we see we're a beautiful flower inside," said the first woman I'd met, named Penny. She was making paper from purple thistle blossoms at Thistle Farms on a sunny morning. Penny lived under a bridge for ten years and couldn't believe that she was now involved in healing others. I couldn't believe she was doing so well either, especially after she took the Tennessee-based *National Geographic* photographer Steven Alvarez and me to see how she had survived, living in a ravine.

Becca Stevens reached out to Penny and hundreds of women like her, in Tennessee and around the world. She will reach out to you in these pages, too, for she is a formidable, beautiful, brilliant woman with an indefatigable faith. Those are wonderful traits in anyone, but I admire them more in people for whom early life "ain't been no crystal stair," as Langston Hughes once put it. As a child she knew loneliness, the betrayal of trust, the senseless shock of grief. All those emotions sent her out to the lawn picking crabgrass, hoping to eradicate a garden scourge. Soon, she realized she couldn't re-create a little Eden. She could, however, find good-luck charms out there in the cul-de-sac wilds of Nashville by "making" four-leaf clovers out of three-leaf clovers and garlanding herself in them. Transformation! But even then, Becca Stevens was utterly one of her own tribe. One of the Magdalene women expected to find her wearing a nun's outfit. Ha! More like "Daisy Duke shorts and a T-shirt." Her husband, Grammy-winning songwriter Marcus Hummon, and her three children have been a constant support.

I was interested to see what role Stevens's mother played here, and was not surprised that she was a beacon. It was her mother, Stevens writes, who told her, as a church builder herself after her husband's death, "to put money into programs, not buildings." Widowed and overwhelmed in a city that was not her own and raising five young children, Stevens's mother depended in part on stoicism. The rawness of life can be its purest essence.

Fate had another blow in store for Stevens. A sexual predator, who happened to be a church elder and family friend, abused her for years. She confronted him eventually— an essential step on her journey not only as a survivor but as an Episcopal priest. Still, that is only part of her story.

Growing up, Stevens also drew strength from mentors and friends, who gave her simplicity and time—which helped her understand the need for healing, an idea that called to her just as it had to her late father during his ministry.

I hope I haven't idealized Becca Stevens. That would be a big mistake. Few people are better for being idealized. She needs to stay close to the work she does, wherever it is, because it teaches her about the strength of a circle of survivors. Between us, Alvarez and I had seen women in ravaged, destitute situations from Afghanistan to Darfur. We met women who described their forced child marriages, their mutilation, rape, torture, and abandonment, every imaginable form of degradation. And yet here were women with tonally identical stories: degraded women here in America, living right beside us, invisible to our eyes.

It's an organic process to be a Thistle Farmer. You start with the kernel of desire for change, and plant it so that it can be harvested. When it sends up shoots, more tending is done, each to each and one to one and all together. So does the mendicant, selling her "snake oil," pour out words of wisdom and forgiveness and experience. Let's call her "snake oil" what it is: her balm of belief, of testimony, and finally, of healing. I was very pleased to be able to tell part of her story on NPR. In *Snake Oil: The Art of Healing and Truth-Telling*, she has told far more of her journey, and those of the women whom Magdalene serves, than I possibly could. This is her gift to you.

Jacki Lyden, host and correspondent, NPR News, and author of *Daughter of the Queen of Sheba*

Introduction

A SNAKE OIL SALESMAN

I<small>T'S KIND OF LIKE</small> selling snake oils."

The words slipped out of my mouth before I could take them back. Did I really just say that out loud?

Being a luncheon speaker is never easy. You're competing with grumbling bellies, clanking forks, and drifting eyes daydreaming about sneaking out early. This noontime gathering for a group of booksellers in Chicago was no exception. I was sharing the story behind Thistle Farms, a not-for-profit women's social enterprise based in Nashville, Tennessee, that employs almost four dozen women. The organization began in 2001 as a program of Magdalene, residential communities that stand in solidarity with women who have survived lives of trafficking, addiction, and prostitution. I explained that for the past twelve years we've made all-natural bath and body care products that we sell with the tagline "love heals." While describing one of the products to the audience, I blurted out, "We basically take the ingredients used in your salad dressing, mix them into a body balm, say a

1

prayer over the blend, and sell the concoction as a healing salve. It's kind of like selling snake oils."

In front of five hundred strangers, I compared myself to a snake oil salesman. The words slipped out, and I quickly moved on with the speech. I'm not sure if anyone paid much attention between finishing the salad and waiting on the entrée. But those accidental words meant something to me. Sometimes a passing thought seems to come from nowhere but, upon reflection, provides a spark of insight on an idea that has been germinating for years. I knew I wasn't the stereotypical portrait of a snake oil salesman selling mixtures out of a dilapidated cart at a state fair. I'm a more modern, social justice–driven version: I select time-tested homemade concoctions and tonics, mix them into an enterprise to help women, and market them as central to healing work that incorporates the body, mind, and spirit.

Reflecting on the term "snake oil salesman" later that afternoon, I realized that though I'd considered the term repulsive for many years, the phrase actually suited me. For thousands of years, healers have handed down the ability to use oils properly. The name derives from the traveling shows out West in the nineteenth century and is rooted in Native American traditions that used the oil from rattlesnakes as powerful medicine to help with rheumatism, arthritis, and other muscle and joint aches. Shamans shared recipes for balms and liniments from rattlesnake oils with early settlers of the American West. Salesmen then got the idea to market the oils from Native Americans and started making all kinds of claims. Thus began the journey of the snake oil salesmen who traveled throughout the West peddling their wares in medicine shows and claiming healing for everything imaginable.

How the oils got such a bad name doesn't lie in the oils themselves. The problem began when people exaggerated the oils' powers and made them into tools to deceive gullible people. As time went on, these "snake oils" contained less and less oil from snakes and more homeopathic tonics filled with ingredients like red pepper and camphor mixed with alcohol—the latter having more to do with the concoctions' soothing effects than the former. Although most of the homeopathic and essential oils necessary for healing were abandoned, these concoctions were still known as "snake oil." The term is now used to refer to a worthless remedy, and a snake oil salesman is one more concerned with making a profit than helping people.

I knew I needed to reclaim the title in a more positive light. After all, I had all the tools I needed to sell the promise of healing. I had a heart full of gratitude, a fair amount of brokenness, a healthy dose of skepticism, a hankering for entrepreneurship, and a big desire to help the underdog. All of those ingredients, mixed with being a priest and an advocate for women on the streets, created a recipe for changing lives.

Instead of laughing the experience off, I wanted to embrace the moment and see where reclaiming the term "snake oil salesman" would lead me in the next few years of work. The comment I made was not meant to devalue the products or their healing abilities, but instead it was intended to offer freedom. The art of healing is a huge gift—the central sacrament a community of faith can offer—yet it is also one of the most abused aspects of the church.

At Thistle Farms we create aromatic and distilled healing oils derived from plants, which in turn we use in our bath and body care products for their therapeutic qualities, as they have been for thousands of years. The oils are the first medicine in history, and the qualities within the oils have potent healing properties that, combined with love and prayers, are a source of healing. Their antiviral, antibacterial, antifungal, and anti-infectious abilities make them valuable tools in the healing process.

Thistle Farms' products have become a means of selling hope and a cause. The products provide healing on many levels—both for those who create them and for those who use them. The products intersect naturally with snake oils because they're made from all-natural ingredients, sold with the intent to heal, and they carry a larger hope with each purchase. Our products have evolved into a line that claims to heal skin, soothe stress, bring women into homes and off the streets, and heal world-weary spirits. The essential oils—including cinnamon and lavender—from which many of the products are derived, provide healing, yet their restorative abilities go beyond their chemical makeup. I find it ironic that I began my career by wanting to be a pastor, separated from the business of the world, and my desire for justice led me to make concoctions that Thistle Farms sells on an open market.

Learning about oils has been like stepping onto an age-old truth and feeling like you are discovering something new. I've never held much stock in those who claim to be faith healers, but I love that I've become part of a faith community that's dedicated to helping people heal both physically and emotionally. I find now that I have more in common with backwoods healers than suburban pastors.

We can all claim to be healers on the journey. That's true for me, and for all of the women I work with. Some of the richest lessons on healing I've learned have come from working side by side making oils with women who have been brutalized in their bodies, have long arrest records, and could use some good oil themselves. The women I began helping fifteen years ago have been the biggest source of my own healing.

One woman is Sara, who at the age of thirteen was sold in Atlanta to an organized group of men who made money selling images on the Internet and servicing men who come to Atlanta for conventions. Now, as the mother of twins, she works hard to manage her health and recovery. The truth she teaches is that healing is not magic. We have to be willing to banish all judgment and love each other in order to heal well. She continues to struggle with the post-traumatic stress that haunts those raped as children and then left to figure out how to survive on their own.

Also women like Penny, the director of the healing oils division, who was raised in a bar and ended up living under a bridge for ten years. Her prayer for years was simply not to wake up beaten or raped. She says the biggest healing experience for her has been the journey to learn to love herself.

These are only two of the hundreds of women I have worked with, and they are powerful teachers that the journey of healing is not a fairy tale but a long story of transformation that inspires us all to keep seeking healing— sometimes even in the most unexpected moments and places. Scores of other women are hoping to find the path of healing. More than one hundred women are on waiting lists to come into one of the community homes at Magdalene.

From this vantage point I am filled with gratitude for all the side roads that led me to the fringes of religious life. These side roads have led me deep into the wilderness, which is where we can learn some of the sweetest lessons about healing and life. Those trails have given me some pretty clear ideas about the role of truth telling in faith healing and the role of economics in a ministry that concerns itself with loving others. Those off-the-beaten-path experiences have given me a bird's-eye view into some of the joys of the healing process and the miracles that unfold on a daily basis in people's lives. And they've led me to take off my blinders to the injustice inherent in our systems and witness some heartbreaking stories. Today, I believe less of the dogma of institutional religion, but what I still believe, I believe more deeply. This journey continues to expand my sense of the undeniable healing power created by the work of love. All this has led me to share in the following pages what I've found to be true. I've included some history of healing oils and the community that makes them, and some recipes so you can make them yourself. I've tried to create a space between snake oils and healing oils, although some overlap is necessary. This is my own blend of storytelling, memoir, and theology.

Healing is as intricate as tatted patterns, as deep as the ocean floor, and as simple as a kiss. But once our eyes and ears are open, stories of healing come in wild waves like flowers blooming on a hillside. For years I walked in hillside parks and never noticed the flower called the trout lily. One spring I noticed a single blossom, and then I saw that there were thousands of them. I wondered how it was possible to not see them. Stories of healing, healers, and snake oils are like that. You may live for years and not see or hear a story of healing, then all of a sudden you hear one that makes you think, and you begin hearing and seeing them all around.

This is a story about love's meandering path. Sometimes in order to heal we go round and round to get a closer look at things. Healing is grounded in four of love's basic axioms: love is eternal, love is sufficient, love is God unfolding in our lives, and love is not concerned with dogma so much as it is a dogged determination to bloom and speak. In fields of lavender, thistle, and lemongrass, I have found love's roots, and I try to nurture them and share their harvest with fellow travelers. The axioms of love are written into the fabric of creation, so it is right that in that fabric we find the gifts we need to heal one another. This circuitous path has led me to being a snake oil salesman of healing oils who helps sustain a community where love can heal.

Chapter One

A CROWN OF CLOVER

Clover Infusion Blend

½ cup fresh dandelions
½ cup fresh clover
3 or 4 fresh mint leaves
1 tablespoon shredded fresh ginger

Rinse the dandelions and clover in a colander. Mix all of the ingredients in a large bowl and set aside. Bring a quart of water to a boil. Remove the water from the heat and pour slowly over the mixture in the bowl, taking deep breaths to breathe in the steam as you pour. The infusion helps with detoxifying and regulating your organs. These common and healing plants gift you with earthy memories and childhood dreams. You will also find that your breathing is

improved and your skin feels soft and supple.
You can buy the mint and ginger from your
local grocery. The dandelions and clover you
can gather in a yard or field; you can use the
leaves, stems, and blossoms of both plants.
Adjust the amount of clover and dandelions
to strengthen or weaken the infusion. Once
it has cooled down, soak a washcloth in the
infused water, place it on your neck and feet,
and enjoy a nice clover wrap!

M Y CONTEMPLATION OF THE universe began with a blade
of crabgrass. I had just turned six and overheard Mr. Price,
a neighbor at the end of the cul-de-sac, talking about getting
rid of all his crabgrass. It was the summer of 1969, and by
all accounts the world had pretty much stalled in mid-orbit
if you judged it by the activities on my dead-end street. But
the world was flying through space and time if I judged it
by how the forces of the universe were acting on us while
we yawned. At the time, my whole world consisted of a tiny
street with my yard as the axis and the place where I began
my journey to understand faith and theology. From there,
I learned the rotation of the earth and the pattern of the
stars, and dreamed of becoming an astronaut—or at least
a gymnast. For me, it was simply a time of living in the
moment, and for the moment I was looking for crabgrass.

To some people on our South Nashville street, crabgrass
was a sign that things were falling apart in the world. In

the late 1960s, integration was well under way, girls were getting ready to become ministers and firemen, and liberals were beginning to make strides against the war, but that all happened outside my tiny world. The biggest problem I faced was trying to find things to do for the summer. I climbed the limbs of the weeping willow tree in the neighbor's yard at least a hundred times. I built a fort of plywood on the lowest branch of one of our silver maples. I played tetherball against the neighborhood kids until my wrists were sore to the touch. I played nighttime tag with a flashlight until all the batteries died. The neighborhood kids accepted that this was our life and that we were all in it together. What made it interesting was the internal thoughts being sown in my heart that would set the course for the rest of my life.

My yard looked boring and average if you judged it by all the other lots in the world, but it was fascinating to me because I knew it like the back of my hand. I loved the two silver maples, the mimosa that Mom said was a junk tree growing through our chain-link fence, and the side yard that spread out between the two. Mr. Price said that crabgrass likes to take over lawns so much that the more desired and fragile grasses never have a chance. When he explained that crabgrass would take over the whole neighborhood if left unchecked, I took it as a personal mission to rid the universe of crabgrass.

Crabgrass is not easy to identify. It changes appearance as it ages and blends in well with the grass and clover of typical lawns. Crabgrass belongs to that strange group of plants we have segregated into the confusing category called weeds. It's an odd classification to me since there were probably no weeds in Eden. Today I think of weeds as invasive and growing spitefully against the will of the people tending the land.

Crabgrass definitely fits into the weed category. The unruly vegetation came with the British and is famed for taking over lawns. As a child, I never questioned crabgrass's classification. If it was a weed, that simply meant it was bad, and our job was to kill it. I never stopped to wonder why God included crabgrass in creation or how the fast-growing grass fit into the idea of healing. Since then I've discovered a hundred beautiful lessons from crabgrass. While we may not want patches of it in our lawn, crabgrass, like all of us, has a rightful place in creation. The roots of crabgrass can be boiled in tea to help with bronchitis. As part of a tonic, crabgrass is a diuretic and hepatic and helpful to both the liver and kidneys. Some even claim that crabgrass will prevent dandruff. None of that was even a passing thought when I was six. I was bored, Mr. Price was sincere, and crabgrass was the enemy.

I ventured into the yard with the sole purpose of searching for the unholy crabgrass, but soon became distracted searching for four-leaf clovers. Finding luck right in the grass proved far more fun than pulling weeds. When I picture myself as a little kid out in the yard, bent close to the earth, searching for a good luck sign that would help heal my family, I imagine that I was bent in quiet contemplation, praying for luck: *Please, O please help me find a four-leaf clover.* I was still child enough to believe that see-ing good luck would soothe my mother's mind. I suppose I also wanted to know there was still order in the world and needed assurance that God had not abandoned us.

My dad, an Episcopal priest, moved to Nashville to start a new church. My mom, a registered nurse from New York, followed with five children in tow. She had never lived in the South, but my mother would move anywhere—including Nashville—for our family. I wanted to find a four-leaf clover before my mother came home from work so I could remind her that everything was going to be all right. She could press the clover between the pages of a book that she had sitting on her bedside table. Maybe in the middle of the night if she woke up worrying about the light bill she would remember the clover by her head and fall back into more pleasant dreams.

My mother was not someone to whom you could offer words of comfort. Like shale, she was full of layers, but impermeable. My mother, who refused to allow anything to break her, kept us at a safe distance from her interior life. I knew she would accept a small gift like a clover, because she loved me, it didn't cost her anything, and she would have known how much I wanted to give it to her.

The previous autumn, the twenty-second of November to be exact, began with my mom saying I could stay home from kindergarten with my little brother to help make a birthday cake for her. It was a normal fall day, neither hot

13

nor cold, and the sky was clear and the kitchen was clean
and aromatic. My sisters all went off to school, and my
brother and I were draped over the couch in the paneled den
while our mother cleaned up around the house. Our small
black Labrador retriever mix, Velvet, nestled nearby on the
shag carpet. I am sure all of those details would have faded
from my five-year-old mind except for what happened next.

My father was scheduled to finish a communion service and then come home to eat lunch with the family. He
decided to visit a couple in crisis on the way, and he called
my mom and promised that as soon as he finished this
pastoral visit, he would be right home. Before hanging up
he wished her happy birthday again.

At eleven thirty in the morning, less than two miles
from our house, a drunk driver in a semitruck struck my
dad's Volkswagen Beetle. A church member who witnessed
the accident raced to our house to deliver the news. My
mom rushed to the hospital, but my dad was already dead.
The accident nearly killed our family as well. It left my
mother struggling to make ends meet with five children in
a Southern city where she had never wanted to live. The
ramifications of that day would ripple through our family
for years, but on the day he died, we still didn't know what
had hit us.

Everyone we knew, along with a few people we'd never
met, began arriving at our house with casseroles in hand
within a few hours of the accident. The table became
the embodiment of people's prayers and love. Those
casseroles—a distant cousin of snake oils—provided medi-

cine for the soul as well as nourishment for the body. The casserole is like a living prayer in the language of the South. Those hot dishes have a scent like the incense priests burned to signify prayers being lifted to the heavens. They're filled with intention, like the poultices shamans mix in sacred bowls.

In the 1960s almost every casserole contained at least one can of Campbell's cream of mushroom soup and crumbled chips or crackers to crisp the top. They were covered with tinfoil to retain their heat. The shiny aluminum sheets gave us a quick mirror image every time we opened the lid. The casseroles were also the incarnation of seasoned and often secret recipes, passed down from sages in the ways of baking. In many ways, the casserole is a sacrament and tool of healing—an outward and visual sign of the inward and spiritual grace of friendship. The act of bringing a casserole to a scene of tragedy, like all sacramental gifts, is profound and good for both the giver and the receiver. An abundance of love is felt in the exchange. The food picks up where words fail us. If a printed prayer to go with casseroles existed, I think it would say something like:

Gracious God, bless this family and keep them going through this stretch. Let them get some sleep and let their stomachs unknot long enough to eat a bite of this casserole. Make sure they feel the time and energy I spent going to the store and getting all the ingredients and cooking and bringing this dish over here, so that they will know I love them. Amen.

The prayers represented by the casseroles carried our family that day and in the weeks that followed. They reminded us that we were in this together and still within reach of God's loving embrace. Regardless of what was unfolding that day, those casseroles were an assurance to my mom that we would still have plenty on our table and that people were watching out for us.

I've learned and relearned as part of the Magdalene community how people find meaning after experiencing suffering and how gifts like casseroles can become a source of healing and deep prayer. Several years ago, I helped bury Lisa's mother. Lisa had been a resident of Magdalene and worked hard to maintain her sobriety. Her family history was filled with suffering exacerbated by the poverty and racism found in rural Tennessee. She was rejected by her father's African American family and raised by her white mother. She grew up poor and ended up on the streets. The day she arrived at Magdalene she was contemplating suicide.

Lisa's mother had been the only person who hadn't abandoned her as a child, and it meant the world to Lisa that her mother lived to see her clean, off the streets, and settled into Magdalene. Lisa was devastated when her mom died. Her mother was buried in the state burial grounds, a place for people who can't afford a plot. When we returned to the Magdalene house after the service, smells of food greeted us at the door with comfort and hope. The frying fish symbolized the abundance of community life. Growing up, Lisa may have been alone and not known where her next meal was coming from, but in the healing community of Magdalene there is always enough to feed everyone. The collard greens and hush puppies were signs that we wanted to offer Lisa love and support. The macaroni casserole with the thick cheese crust brought us all back to our roots.

I have no idea who brought the food to our house the day my father died. At three feet tall, I could see only the dresses, not faces. Those dresses blended into a vision that looked like a clothesline of women, descendants of the faithful from all religions who gather in death to comfort and wail. The colors of the dresses are strung together in my mind like Tibetan prayer flags. Men filled our house that day as well, loving and caring for the family. I was hiding in the kitchen, though, so I remember the women most vividly.

Yet as Christmas approached and people went back to their busy lives, we were left to figure out how to make a life and living. I felt so sad for my mother, who carried the grief alone. She didn't complain to us, but you could read how the pain was leading her like a map. I would have done anything in the world to take that pain away from her, but it was beyond my reach. My throat still clenches whenever I think about my mother and her brood of children trying to make it those first few years.

The experience made me suspicious of the notion of miracles. It's not uncommon for people to say to those in crisis that they're praying for a miracle. But I always thought that if God handed those out, God would have given us one that day. I never felt like God had abandoned us, but I learned that God's presence didn't guarantee a miracle was forthcoming. I believed that my priestly father was faithful and died in the act of service. Since healing didn't translate into saving his life, I reckoned that God didn't miraculously heal people. I always felt that when people talked about healing, they were talking about a paralyzed person being able to walk again or that my father would just all of a sudden start breathing again on the operating table. People were just blowing smoke when they talked that way. I had no idea at the time how there could be healing in death and how healing could be deeper and stronger than the supposed miracle cures I had seen on television. The experience of losing my father made faith more about how I was going to live my life than about how God was going to affect the daily activities before me.

That experience was formative and set me on a path I didn't even know I was walking—one paved with the truth that faith and healing are more about actions than words. Even though no one held a secret formula to spare us from pain or trouble, we could get through it. I discovered that faith was simply the strength to keep walking, even when taking the next step seems impossible. That path also helped me see that a desire for faith was a sign of faith itself. I didn't have to understand the meaning of the suffering we went through; I could just get through it all and trust that the meaning of suffering would come in hindsight. On the path I was walking, my faith was not going to be tested by suffering. My faith was going to ground me as I walked through suffering in the world. On the path, I could rest assured that even though I trembled in the valley of the shadow of death, I was still walking with God.

Maybe that's one reason I spent so much time alone mulling about in the yard, hunting crabgrass and four-leaf clovers. Grieving and searching are two of the oldest elements of healing. As ancient as the mountains and the rivers, they form the place where Moses stood, where the Buddha sat under the Bodhi tree, where Jesus wept in the garden, and where we still go to find hope. The first pages of scripture give us a vision of a garden called Eden that holds a tree of life. The last pages of scripture allow us to glimpse the long-awaited city of God. In the middle of the city, on the banks of a river, another tree of life appears, one whose leaves are made for the healing of the world. The leaves of this tree drip with oil; its bark can be made into teas and its roots can be ground and eaten as an eternal gift. The tree of life, a source of healing, bookends the vision of God's kingdom and reminds us that healing is sewn into the very fabric of creation. Its roots run deep beneath our feet. I can see now that those same roots were running under me in my childhood and even embedded in my yard.

I was connecting myself to the people who for thousands of years have used snake oils and herbs to create healing medicines for their communities. In China, ancient records indicate that small amounts of ointments containing venom have been used in healing for centuries. The oils, made from the Chinese water snake, were said to heal joint pain. Meanwhile, Egyptians used oils from adders to stop pain and heal skin infections. On the other side of the world, Native Americans have used plants and herbs to make healing teas, tinctures, and salves. Some Native Americans tribes collected and used traces of essential oil from the leaves of white clover to make teas, tonics, and all kinds of remedies.

My father's death connected me to the eternal grief that has thrown everyone out into their yard at one time or another. His death also connected me to the eternal healing that was within my grasp. In the yard, I forgot about the stress created by the vacuum of his absence. After forgetting about crabgrass and never finding a four-leaf clover, I made a delicate crown of clovers by tying the end of one stem to the flower of the next. I wore the flowery crown like a princess until one of my older sisters told me to take it off and help get dinner ready before Mom came home. I paused to admire my work. By placing the crown on my stringy, dirty-blond hair, I had made myself feel beautiful, and as far as I can think back, that was the first anointing I remember doing. While I created that crown of flowers, I was free to daydream about endless possibilities. In the yard, my faith found root. I discovered strength for my weary soul as my body drank in the vitamin D from the sunshine.

Years later I discovered that clovers too are full of healing. Those oval-shaped leaves are full of tannins useful for cleaning wounds and disinfecting the skin. I sometimes wonder if even as a child, somewhere in my heart, I knew that I had so many wounds that needed cleaning that I couldn't help but be drawn toward the clover leaf. I never imagined that hunting crabgrass and clovers was part of the training for my road ahead.

Chapter Two

AN OLD BITTER PILL

Geranium Blend

4 ounces aloe vera oil*
14 drops geranium essential oil
12 drops grapefruit essential oil
8 drops lemongrass essential oil
6 drops golden champa essential oil
(expensive, so optional)

Pour all of the ingredients into a glass
container and mix thoroughly; the essential
oils come in small vials with tops designed
to pour out in drops. Whisk the ingredients
for about 30 seconds to combine. This is a
tried-and-true recipe that acts as a bug

* In each recipe the first ingredient is given in ounces because
it is the carrier oil that holds the essential oils measured in drops.

repellant. Rub this on your ankles and wrists
before you head out into the wilderness.
The blend also smells wonderful, is great for
clarity, and opens your heart to prayer. The
essential oils and the carrier oil, aloe vera,
can be found in stores that specialize in all-
natural foods and natural body products. Or
you can purchase them online from any one
of a number of companies that sell "certified"
essential oils.

I HATED GOING TO church. My dad had taken a job at a
podunk mission and moved us all to the South because he
wanted to help plant a new congregation. I didn't understand his vision or dream. Instead, all I saw was a shoebox-
size brick building on a poorly maintained road. The scene
was depressing. I struggled to wrap my head around the
idea that he had lost his life in service of it. After his death,
my mom gave away almost everything he had, except for a
few personal things. The one thing that she gave me was
his *Book of Common Prayer*. To this day, I don't have a single sermon he wrote, any of his theological volumes, or the
records of his service as a pastor. I have only his prayer book.

That well-worn red prayer book has taught me more
about his life of faith than anything else. The book includes
Pastoral Offices, which are the religious rites and ceremo-
nies performed by priests, including marriages, baptisms,
and weekly communion services. The pages for the religious

rites, which my dad used weekly, were all intact. But the pages for private daily prayer services were held together by strips of clear tape. Those pages speak volumes about my father's interior life. They tell me that it wasn't the public services he led, but the private services he prayed every morning and every night of his short life, that wore out the pages.

One day early in my ministry I picked up the book and a small note slipped out that was written on a scrap of paper. It read, "In the shadow of his cross, may your soul find rest," in my father's handwriting, and I believe the line was from a sermon he both preached and needed to hear. On the day those words fell from the prayer book, it felt like an answered prayer: a sign that that my dad was peaceful in the shadow of the cross, and that he died doing what he loved. The words were healing. When I was growing up my father's death seemed like a sad ending for a priest with great aspirations and talent. The congregation he led struggled to keep the doors open and pay the bills after his death. While faithful in attendance and sincere in worship, the church lacked a vision for being a loving and healing presence in the world.

A friend of my father's attended the same church. I hated him. At the time, I didn't know why. He was a church elder. When my father died, this man stepped in under the guise of being a good friend to the family. None of us realized that he was a predator who took full advantage of our mom's trust for years. I thought this religious man was faithful, powerful, and trustworthy. He sported slicked-back black hair and thick, black-rimmed glasses, and underneath he was as oily as you can imagine. An average man in height and weight, he stood tall and strong in my memory.

This man was a snake oil salesman in the worst sense of the phrase. He offered us venom that we bought like liquid gold. He sold us a mirage and preyed on my innocence. He represents the villain in the story of my childhood, the purveyor of concoctions made by people who gain power on the backs of the suffering. The abuse I endured was confusing to me. He showed generosity and kindness to my family. Then, when everyone was gone, he would hold me down or hold me in his lap. He was oily and so strong that he could hold me in any position so I couldn't move. I didn't know how to respond. In those moments I felt as if concrete were being poured down the back of my throat. My body felt heavy and my mind would drift off.

The first incident took place in the fellowship hall of the church during a spaghetti supper. I have no idea why no one knew or why I didn't tell. I've since discovered that this is a common experience among abused children. You know it's wrong, but it feels that if you acknowledge it your whole world might fall apart. The abuse went on periodically for two years.

I remember the last time he abused me. Both of our families drove out to the countryside. It was a happy day, and I was thrilled that I was getting a chance to ride a horse. By the time I realized that he and I were alone in the barn, it was too late. My mom had just left from the far end of the stable toward the riding ring. He picked me up, carried me on his hip, and walked toward the other end of the barn.

I can still smell the stink of the horse stall. Thick straw and a few piles of manure coated the concrete floor. Once inside the stall, he closed the wooden door with the X pattern of the reinforcing timber. I was completely hidden. The pungent smell of dung and damp straw dulled all the other senses that wanted to overwhelm me. I stared at him with a blend of fear, anger, and hate. The details of that final scene of abuse—the scent and paralyzing fear—have remained vivid in my memory, as colorful and detailed as an oil painting.

I still don't know why he stopped abusing me after that day. Maybe I had finally learned to keep away, maybe the way I stared him down worked, or maybe I just had gotten too big for him to pick up. Like many abused kids, I thought I had done something to trigger the abuse, and I would feel humiliated if anyone knew what I had let him do to me. To this day, talking and writing about the abuse feels like a betrayal to his family and the community I came from. I still worry about who might get mad about me writing it all down. Yet telling the truth of abuse and sharing the story are essential parts of my healing.

The abuse taught me some valuable lessons, and I paid a high price for each one. One of those lessons was that I don't have to trust authority. I can move around it, disregard it, or even use it to my advantage. That gift has served me well in my work, except for my nervousness when dealing with church hierarchy. For a long time I didn't know how to engage authority without feeling strange and untrusting. I thought that working under authority was full of land mines and traps, and as soon as I was dumb enough to slip up, I'd lose my legs. I had to trust my own authority and intuition, and find my own way. This lesson provided the strength to start the Magdalene community and work with a model of shared authority.

This past year a woman named Shana came into Magdalene with the words "Trust no one" tattooed on her chest. I thought about how sad and hard those words are to bear as a young woman. But lately I have been thinking that they can be a gift to her. She can read those words and remember that she can trust herself. When she can't trust anyone else, she can trust her own voice.

It took me decades and the experience of starting the Magdalene community to understand that if I wanted to serve and be a part of the healing journey for others, I needed to get on with my own healing process. There would be stories and incidents that would trigger memories, and it was hard to do the work. One day, after running into the man who abused me at a wedding ceremony, where he tried to hug me as if everything were fine between us, I finally decided it was time to call his house. I needed to talk with my abuser. It was scary to call, but I knew if I wanted to serve others I needed to stop carrying around my own wounds like precious pearls. I had to give them back to the man who abused me.

During the phone call I explained to his wife that I wanted to come over that evening and talk with both of them. The whole situation was difficult and awkward as we sat down in their living room.

I began by addressing his wife. "I have a story to tell you," I said. "Your husband abused me when I was a child."

The wife clenched her stomach and went to the bathroom to vomit. As we waited for her to come back into the room, he rubbed his hand back and forth on his thigh like he was a nervous wreck. After another few awkward minutes she came back into the living room and I began to talk.

"I don't care," I said. "I don't care if you cry or get sick. I need to tell you the story of what happened to me when I was a young girl and then tell you what you need to do about it." The man admitted his guilt. He said he had wanted to talk with me about the abuse, but didn't know how to bring it up.

The first question he asked startled me: "Who have you told?"

"Anyone I wanted to," I replied. "It's not my secret."

I asked them not to have any contact with me; it was just too hard. I told them what I had learned about how abusers don't heal without help and gave them a list of programs that he could call for assistance. I told his wife that contact with their small grandchild without help and supervision would be considered endangerment. I left saying that I would pray for them and that from my vantage point there was plenty of grace that was needed by all. I have forgiven him and pray that he found help.

Another lesson the abuse taught me was that I could learn more from mercy than judgment. One of the results of the abuse was that I made a lot of mistakes. I made some poor decisions about relationships—a natural outcome of sexualizing young girls. I remember one time I drank at a camp and was sent home without anyone asking me where I got the alcohol or why I drank so much. I needed mercy. Another time, after I was threatened by my high school boyfriend, I walked to my church and went into the pastor's office and told him I was scared. The priest sat across from me as I cried and listened to the whole story. Then he told me that the church was a safe place and I could always come in and just sit. He was mercy in the flesh. I needed people like that priest to not ask too many questions and to forgive me when I got angry too fast, when I acted a bit crazy, or when I got scared and ran. Love is most radical when offered without judgment and given with a sense of gratitude for all the mercy that has been afforded to us.

Another valuable lesson I learned through my abuse is that healing takes time. Just as soaking in the goodness of oils on a regular basis takes time and diligence, so too inner healing is a lifelong journey, not a magical cure. I've known people who gave up using homeopathic oils because the effects are slow and subtle, and I've known people who gave up on seeking healing from the events of the past—including abuse—because of the time and patience required. I've seen women over the years take the long road toward healing.

Regina, one of the first residents of Magdalene, talks about how her road to respecting and loving herself took her more than ten years. During all of those years she served others as outreach director and simply believed that one day she would feel well. She says that even after sixteen years of living clean, she still has days when she wonders how much more work she has in front of her to heal from the violence and addiction she survived. I think that she is as strong and beautiful a woman as I have ever known. The stronger she gets, the brighter the whole world looks to me.

In the early years of my priesthood I spent a few summers leading groups of teens to Rosebud Reservation in South Dakota. During those summers I began to appreciate how important determination and patience are in healing. We went through weeklong classes about their traditions and values, and then spent a few days attending a large pow-wow. The first morning of the powwow, we set out early to find seats. We watched for hours as people entered and slowly prepared the place for the gathering. The dancers finally arrived, and the drumming began. As we watched, dancers began to move in small, slow, rhythmic steps. The drumming grew louder but never faster.

For several hours, the slow dance continued around the circle. People stood up to talk and eat. I finally realized I wasn't going to miss a big finale if I got up to move around. When I returned to my seat, I relaxed and began to think of the movements as more of a trance than a dance. The dancers continued into the night and picked up the next day where they had ended. Some of our group, feeling like they had already experienced the powwow, remained by the campsite most of the day, but the rest of us made our way back and watched people move in a circle to the drums for another two days.

Years later, I learned that part of the reason for the dance is to bore the bad spirits so they will cross over the mountains and leave. I saw the powwow in my mind and thought about how we had wanted to leave. In staying we were opening ourselves up to transformation and healing. The journey to healing is usually not fast—it's a slow dance.

My healing journey has taken thousands of prayers, countless small bites of bread, and gallons of wine one sip at a time. Slowly and surely I hear the rhythms of the drums beating in time with my own heart. The abuse taught me that I could trust my own voice and be patient in the healing process, and that the mercy I experienced in my life was stronger than judgment. These lessons all played important roles as I reached out to serve others.

I attended a small liberal arts college in the mountains of Tennessee on a scholarship and majored in mathematics. All of my sisters, brilliant and beautiful, were married by the time they were eighteen, but I knew that I needed to get away and get to the mountains. I went through the normal ups and downs at the school, including a couple bouts of depression. I spent a summer interning in Coventry, England.

After graduating I moved to Washington, DC, to work for Bread for the World, an organization founded by a Lutheran pastor named Art Simon, who believed there were enough resources in the world to feed all the children who were hungry. He said we didn't lack resources, but the spirit to share them. During the year I lived in our nation's capital, I realized that while I loved working on issues around justice and community, I wanted to do it from a faith community, not just through community organizing. I met a female priest, a fairly rare occurrence in 1986, and she inspired me to think that maybe I could get through the ordination process. I also felt that if I didn't start graduate school soon, I never would. After I spent some time working in the hills of North Carolina, I moved home and went to Vanderbilt Divinity School on a scholarship.

I had no desire to stay in Nashville, but it made sense to go back and live with my mom to get a master's of divinity degree and see if the diocese of Tennessee would let me go through the rigorous ordination process. During the first week of divinity school, I met my husband, Marcus Hummon, one of the greatest gifts of my life. I was still pretty skittish in relationships, and when he asked me out I had my doubts. I had landed a job running a transitional housing program for families. One of the families had abandoned their house and left a bunch of furniture infested with crab lice. I asked Marcus if he wanted to go with me to load up the furniture for the dump. He said yes and never complained, and I felt that in addition to being beautiful and a wonderful musician, he was strong and trustworthy. We were married the next fall.

During this time the idea of starting a sanctuary for women to live in was germinating. I didn't like the way the women on the streets were being treated by the very systems that had been set in place to help them.

Before I opened the first home, I started visiting

women in jails and ran into more people I knew than I had expected. I met jailers, attorneys, counselors, and prisoners with whom I had graduated from high school. One woman who came to Magdalene was someone I remembered from childhood. She had been abused during those years by a horrible neighbor, and despite all her efforts at getting away from him, she ended up on the streets about four miles from where she grew up, exchanging sex with abusive men for drugs, living the nightmare over and over. While visiting women in jail, I also met women who sat teary-eyed as they listened to other women describe their harrowing stories. I haven't met anyone walking the streets of my hometown who has not been raped. I thought I was going to the jail to meet strangers, and I met myself.

Placing the act of serving women within the context of my own life and in the larger context of history grounds the story and gives it depth and strength. Many times the places and people we are moved to serve arise from the places and events in our past that have been broken. Recognizing and being mindful of that brokenness moves us toward compassion and service. If our own brokenness is moving us toward controlling or obsessing, though, it is not a good idea for anyone. We have had to pay close attention to brokenness in our community. Most of the residents, volunteers, and staff arrive at the community of Magdalene not because it's all gone so well, but because their brokenness has given them empathy for each other's suffering. In the community we have to be mindful that in serving one another we are not just projecting our own pain onto each other.

To offer our story in connection with a larger story reminds us that we are not alone and that all our stories are related. That larger context can be our grounding or our undermining. When it is our undermining, we are carrying the brokenness from one generation into another like a simple link in a chain. When it is our grounding, we are remembering that the larger story is that love survives, and that we are grounded in love first and foremost. When we are grounded in the larger context we have a right and a privilege to claim knowledge and to speak that truth wherever we wish. We have a right to an opinion on faith that may be different from that of the people in authority. It is hard to think that through prayer and action you have to come to a different conclusion about what faith means. It's even harder to try to share that truth in a respectable and compassionate way with those we love.

Over the years, about two hundred women have graced the doorstep at Magdalene and come to live as residents in the program. More than seventy-two percent of the women have been clean and sober two and a half years after they come in. For most of the women, their first memories are of trauma, and the horror stories never seem to end. The doors of the first house at Magdalene were finally opened the second week of August 1997. It took two years to get the board organized and raise enough money to be a viable charitable organization. People donated a house, painted it, found the resources we needed to access doctors and therapists, and took care of the paperwork and books. The women who came into the program were strong and took leadership of the community immediately.

I remember meeting with the women right after they moved in and explaining my hope about the healing nature of community. One of the women didn't agree with me, and I thought her response to me was a little aggressive. I told her that there was no reason for her to get upset. She stood up and leaned over me and with her finger in my face said, "You haven't seen me upset." I believed her! I let her know that it was fine by me if we just waited to see how it could be a safe home for her. My role after the house opened was to make sure the bills were paid, keep the community close to its foundation, organize outreach and education, and go by in the evenings to check on the women and make sure everyone was safe.

One evening in early September I drove by and caught sight of Regina, one of the residents, dancing in the living room. I pulled the car over to see what kind of party was going on in the house. She was alone dancing to Gospel music. She was moving to the Spirit and dancing with joy. We talked for a minute, then I returned to my car and wept. The tears flowed, in part because I didn't remember the last time the Spirit had moved me to dance. I wanted to feel that kind of joy moving in my life. I longed for the intimacy of faith Regina felt. I wanted to know the depth of a faith that prompted my father to write, "In the shadow of his cross, may your soul find rest." I wanted to know what healing felt like in the cavern of my heart.

Chapter Three

SEEDS OF HEALING

Tea Tree Blend

3 ounces olive oil
10 drops tea tree essential oil
10 drops sweet orange essential oil
6 drops patchouli essential oil
4 drops peppermint essential oil

Pour all of the ingredients into a glass
container and whisk to combine. You can
enjoy this oil all over your body. The blend
is great for when you feel anxious, or when
you are suffering from an achy cold. The
patchouli oil helps treat everything from
athlete's foot to eczema and dermatitis. Tea
tree oil is a gift that helps heal infections and
acne, and boosts overall immunity. Peppermint
oil, with its menthol, is an analgesic for

muscle aches. Once the blend is absorbed into the skin, it makes its way through the bloodstream, providing healing on the inside and outside. For sore backs or legs, the addition of a prayerful massage is a huge gift. The olive oil can come from the shelf of your local grocery. Many stores that specialize in all-natural foods carry the essential oils.

IF MR. OILY WAS the crabgrass, then Mr. Price was the sweet clover and the first good snake oil salesman I had ever met. This neighbor worked his whole life for the government making road maps of Tennessee. He drove a shiny pick-up truck that he waxed on Saturdays in his driveway. The bumper sticker on the back boasted that you could pry his gun from his cold, dead hands. Even as his hair grayed and thinned, he was always busy in his yard or working on things in his garage. I never remember seeing him tired.

Mr. Price taught me how to bait a hook at Percy Priest Lake in Nashville and told me there were nests of baby copperheads in the bottom of the lake that once swarmed a young girl who jumped off a rope swing. I knew he was kidding, but the thought kept me in the boat and on my toes. He was a great father figure to me—keeping me safe and making me laugh. On my birthday, he took me to O'Charley's restaurant, and I ordered a sirloin steak with A.1. sauce, the fanciest meal I can remember having as a child.

This kind neighbor is the first person I think of when I think of purveyors of good snake oil, not the nasty snake oil salesmen who sold bridges to people in the desert, but fun snake oil sellers who mixed up crazy tonics with the hope you'd feel better with a bit of luck. Even to this day, Mr. Price is a kind of memory tonic I take when I need to feel grounded and loved.

Mr. Price specialized in homemade remedies. Anything he could find lying around was fair game. Whenever a bee or wasp stung me, Mr. Price wet tobacco and placed it over the sting. If I cut myself while playing, he used a cloth dipped in turpentine to cleanse the wound. For scrapes, he used handkerchiefs dipped in mysterious concoctions he kept in his basement. For stomachaches, he handed me a peppermint. He made use of baking soda, apple cider vinegar, tobacco, witch hazel, paper, lard, and anything else around the house that he knew would ease pain.

When I was growing up, Mr. Price seemed to have the ability to make just about anything better—whether fixing a flat tire or spicing up a boring day. He'd whip out his pocketknife and begin to carve a peach pit and the world felt like a better place. He had a clothesline in his backyard, which he used as a place to grow grapes. In the fall, we'd crush them with our bare feet. Whenever I had the blues, he had an inappropriate joke that made me laugh. He took pride in me as if I were his own, and despite his tough exterior, he was one of the gentlest creatures God ever made.

Mr. Price carried around a private catalog of old wives' tales. He recounted his days of growing up poor and all of the things that his mother and grandmother did to heal him and keep him going. He was patient in his teaching, and even though his mouth was full of dentures, his smile was beautiful. When he was in a really funny mood, he would pop his top denture out and smile. His deeper teachings about friendship, loyalty, and compassion for the under-dog as well as all of his practical knowledge—how to turn grapes into wine, how to stop a sting with tobacco, and how to use oil from a can to heal scars—have stuck with me throughout my life.

After school most days, I walked down to Mr. Price's house and we'd sit. He let me take draws off the pipe he smoked. He didn't mind that I was a six-year-old girl. He thought it showed strength of character that I could smoke and not cough at all. He'd pass the pipe and say matter-of-factly, "You shouldn't smoke." Yet he always offered, and I always accepted.

I savored the feel of the ivory stem of the pipe resting warm on my mouth. I enjoyed the sweet scent of his cheap tobacco, and I loved that I was brave enough to smoke. Sometimes I think that it made me a bit numb to some of the pain I carried around. I think it's interesting that five hundred years ago people used tobacco for almost every ailment under the sun. People eventually realized the toxic properties in the nicotine, but the external use of tobacco on stings and bites remains. Tobacco has been a mainstay in rituals of cleansing and worship across more time and space than I can imagine, and because of Mr. Price, tobacco has always been in my life. Some nights even now, after everyone has gone to bed, I'll sit out on my porch and smoke a cigarette. I have gone through periods without smoking, but it seems to always play a role in my life—maybe it's a reminder of Mr. Price.

Each family on our dead-end street had their own stories and troubles to combat. The Harris family owned a dog named Satan who earned his name by terrorizing us at random times for no apparent reason. The messiest neighbors were the Willie family. They didn't throw trash around so much as they didn't clean up after the neighborhood kids, and we were pretty much feral children making a mess wherever we played. Mr. Moser had a good yard because after he was paralyzed from a tsetse fly bite he got in Africa, he would ride his lawnmower most of the day. The Brown family had a nice yard, but they argued a lot. A friend once told me that their dad would get really mad sometimes, so I was afraid of them. The Destefano family lived next door to us. Their uncle made Italian lamps in their basement. Because they had fruit trees in their yard, we all had to stay off their property. Finally, there was the Quarrel family—fittingly named, since the dad was mean as hell when he drank.

With the exception of Mr. Price, no one in the neighborhood ever seemed to think about anointing another person in a healing way. In our neighborhood, we kids were raised to not be sissies and to find ways to entertain ourselves, but still we managed to find sweetness in it all—the smell of the magnolia trees, the taste of the honeysuckle, the brush of branches from the weeping willows we ran through. Beautiful things, like clover in crabgrass, captured our hearts and hopes for the future. We all knew enough to take time out and anoint ourselves with things like clover crowns, stolen fruits, and tobacco poultices to help us feel better and remind us that we were valuable and beautiful. During long summer days, we'd run free around the neighborhood searching for something or making up crazy games until someone's mom yelled that it was time to go home. Searching for something beautiful or creating an imaginary world was as natural as breathing. I wonder if all children, given the freedom, search for beauty wherever they are.

I've seen kids in the poorest neighborhoods of South Africa and developing parts of the globe laughing as they kick up the dirt while playing soccer with a ball made from wadded up plastic bags. I've watched kids from just about every continent create castles in dirt and sand, music from their hearts, and magic from sunlight and water. Poverty doesn't end imagination, suffering doesn't stop hope in children, and healing is just as universal and instinctual for kids as ducking when someone yells, "Heads up!" Seeing the resiliency of children reminds us all to never give up on our own healing. Children remind us to explore and celebrate life, and even the most mundane details of life can become a source of joy.

*　　*　　*

Healing also seemed within reach because I grew up with a medicine cabinet consisting of an old cardboard box underneath the sink in my mom's bathroom. Growing up, I never thought of healing as something performed by a stranger in a lab coat, but a permeable offering that changed depending what was available in the box. Healing was an art that used homemade concoctions. That old, stained cardboard box contained hundreds of escaped Q-tips cluttering the contents along with half-empty bottles of aspirin. All sizes of Band-Aids lined the box, along with Benadryl in every form available. The usual suspects included NyQuil, Neosporin, and some old antibiotics my mom kept from past illnesses just in case. Some of my mom's friends who were pharmaceutical representatives handed out free samples; Mom kept them and then used them sparingly whenever we became ill. My mom, who was trained as an RN, wasn't above going to the doctor; she just had a lot of confidence in her own ability to take care of us. Her medicine cabinet was our own medical clinic.

The cardboard box didn't keep office hours or send us bills. We learned early on how to get better on our own. The few times I went to the doctor I felt like it irritated her—partly because she had to take time off work, and also because it meant that she was not able to care for us herself. Her practicality was simple and useful, and we were a pretty healthy litter of kids under her care. When we were sick, Mom prepared cinnamon toast for us, made us sip

41

Coke, and let us stay on the couch all day without having to share the cushions with siblings. When she came home from work, she would have a small present to make us feel better. I thought she was a great nurse.

I never remember my mom using a thermometer. She simply placed her hands on our foreheads, waited a minute, and then told us whether or not we were sick. She would also take our temperature every time she came through the room by giving us a long kiss on the forehead. She would declare as she left the room, "I think you're getting a little better." That is a beautiful image of the practice of healing to me—to have a kiss from someone who loves you and tells you that you are a little better. Her simplicity and purposefulness made her a good healer for us. She was not afraid of practicing any kind of medicine. One of the neighborhood kids had cystic fibrosis, and she went to their house every afternoon and administered a shot and breathing treatments to help him. She also removed all the stitches in the neighborhood and taped one of the Willie children's fingers back when he almost lost a digit on the swing set. Because of her quick and calm action, they reattached the finger at the hospital. To this day, I've never bothered to buy a thermometer.

Sometimes I think we make healing too complicated. Healing can be as simple as a kind word, a healing salve from a medicine box, or laying our hands on someone and offering a prayer. Part of the art of healing comes from practical study and listening, from a pure heart and a fearless desire to reach out and ease the suffering of others.

The oils are one of the best tools we have to carry on that journey. They help us keep it simple. I inherited the instinct to want to heal and to do it simply, artfully, and with prayer from my mother. I learned from Mr. Price to use all the ordinary tools that we have around us to create something magical. All those lessons are foundational in the practice of selling oils and becoming a healer.

My instinct to blend crafts, social justice, and healing never left me. I am as excited today about finding a new product and listening to a new story as I was when I started. Living on that dead-end street was the beginning of my lesson about the importance of sanctuary in healing. We all need a safe place. We need to be surrounded by people who will encourage us, help find salve for our wounds, and climb out on a limb with us.

That's one reason I was so passionate about establishing the Magdalene community. Mary Magdalene was the name of the first person to preach about resurrection, and she experienced deep healing from old wounds. In the accounts of the resurrection stories offered in the Gospels, it seems like in each story Jesus lingers to meet Magdalene. In the account of the resurrection in the Gospel of John, two disciples run into the tomb and see the shroud that Jesus had been wrapped in. They leave scared, and Magdalene is left alone. As she stands outside the tomb, she bends over to look into the tomb. Jesus speaks to her. The bond and power of grace seem to bring her into the heart of God. I wanted to name the community in her honor and for it to be a sanctuary. I knew that in order to heal people, women needed a place to speak their truth in love without fear of being judged, in part because I needed that place. I took all that I had learned from the old neighborhood, combined it with the knowledge and experience I gained from school and work, and developed the model of a healing community.

When we opened our first home and invited five women who had been on the streets or in jail for years to live there, we began with the premise that we wanted to be a witness to the truth that grace offered freely could heal some of the deepest wounds of the world. For me, it was important that Magdalene offered a place for women with no strings attached. No one has to sign a lease to live in one of the six Magdalene residences. I knew from my abuse that it's hard to trust authority, and so no one on staff or anyone with authority lives in any of the houses. I have never had a key to any of the Magdalene homes. I have to knock on the door and ask to come in.

More than anything, I wanted Magdalene to be a lavish gift to the women, the city, and me. Growing up poor taught me that a home is a huge gift. When I was a child, a flat tire was a disaster, and all five of us knew to scatter whenever it was time for our mother to pay the bills. Whenever appliances broke, she placed patterned contact paper over the front of them instead of replacing them. For years she stored dishes in a broken dishwasher covered in yellow contact paper. The clothes washer was covered in flowered contact paper. To use the machine, she held the hose that drained the water over a bucket. She would have to start and stop the rinse cycle several times to empty the bucket in the sink. After working all day, standing by the washer for the entire rinse cycle must have been a pain.

That's why providing homes for two years to the women in the Magdalene program is so important. Many of the women have been stressed about money much of their lives. Magdalene offers every woman a place to live well without having to cover broken appliances with contact paper. We furnished the homes with new, matching furniture. The thought behind having new furniture and working appliances is that they are the outward and visible sign of self-worth. They provide a tangible incarnation of how we experience being children of God.

From the people I loved growing up, including my mom and Mr. Price, I discovered the other qualities the communities should embody. The Magdalene homes needed to be creative, practical, and joyful. They needed to be sanctuaries where women were absolutely safe, not just physically, but mentally and emotionally safe enough to follow their own instincts toward healing. Magdalene would be known for its sweet healing gardens, beautiful baskets, and thick new comforters. After the first few homes opened, I began to understand more clearly how the abuse I experienced connected me to the vast majority of the women I served. Let me be clear: I am not comparing the abuse I went through to the terrifying stories I have heard over the years from women who have survived life on the streets. Sometimes I don't know how my friends at Magdalene survived their childhood. My experiences pale in comparison to the

suffering I have heard about, but they allowed me to con-
nect and develop a model that is a lavish, intimate testimony that in the end, love and grace are the most powerful
forces for social change in the world. Magdalene has taught
me that if we are given the luxury of time, space, and community, we can find a healing path. The path we find may
be as far as from here to Tibet, we may have to walk it on
our knees, and we may not have a great map, but we will
have access to it.

Over the years I have watched the healing process take
root in women as they dwell in a safe place with time to
recover. Their words start to have a lilt to them like when
a dandelion starts to sway in a field because the wind picks
up. Their steps get a bit faster because they have somewhere
to go.

Jennifer is a beautiful woman from Ohio who came to
our community after her priest found us online. She arrived
broken and ragged. I remember that her strawlike hair
hadn't been dyed in months and her teeth were pretty
rough. But those were just details anyone could see from
the outside. The deeper story was one of rape and abuse
that she had been running from for thirty-five years.

When she arrived her face was unflinching and her
words were flat, yet she says God heard her cry for help.
She says that she didn't even know that she was healing
the first few months that she was in the community. She
recalls moments where something dawned on her, and she
began to make a connection between her past and present,
but she can't pinpoint the exact moment when she started

loving herself or her life. Jennifer says that she can see the healing looking back, but she didn't feel it taking root as she went through it in real time. The hope of being with her children again and wanting desperately to feel joy kept her going. As I shared my own story with her, she too could see places in her life where she made her own crowns of clover and found places of healing, even as she was going through a terrible hell. Bonds deepen whenever people share stories with one another. Now she says her three favorite times of the week are her hour with her therapist, the time she is making thistle paper at work, and all the time she spends in prayer. If you see her quiet and smiling, she is in prayer and living a free life.

As women began arriving at Magdalene to find healing in a safe place and with each other, I realized the need for something more. All the women came from the streets, prison, or both. They had huge gaps in their education, serious addictions, long arrest records, and little work history. All of that meant that most of the women couldn't land a job. Though they were getting clean and healing, the women were financially unstable. Healing isn't just physical, emotional, and spiritual, but also economic.

More needed to be done to help the residents of Magdalene find jobs and develop marketable skills, and to encourage education. But the work needed to be something that walked hand in hand with healing in body, mind, and spirit.

*　　*　　*

My bathtub is a 1940s tub with four handles, the kind that looks like they added a shower sometime after they put in the tub. It's a small old tub, but it is one of the best sanctuaries I have in this world. After I had my third son, I spent untold hours in that tub bathing my baby and found it to be a refuge after the rest of the family went to bed. It was while I was spending time in the tub that the idea of making bath and body care products came to life. I started playing with salts and mixing fragrances, and one day the thought occurred to me that I could make some of the oils part of my work. I could share what I found to heal myself with a community in search of healing—then that community could extend healing to others.

We decided to make aromatic and healing balms, once upon a time known simply as snake oils. They became a means by which women could heal from life on the streets while offering healing to people who bought them. It was from this space that the idea of Thistle Farms came to life almost twelve years ago. About ninety percent of the women who were residents were unemployed, and we needed to start a workplace where women could become economically independent. We began simply, but since then we've made hundreds of blends and used many plants and tonics in our healing products.

The women of Magdalene, on average, were first sexually abused between the ages of seven and eleven. I have never met a woman from the streets of Nashville who has not been raped. Every woman who works at Thistle Farms needs meaningful and dignified work. They, like me, needed to heal in body, mind, and spirit, and all-natural products with good essential oils help us remember that our bodies are a gift and that they can be healthy. The products are a way to take our story, of hope and truth telling about why women are on the streets and how they come back into the wider community, to a larger audience.

In making and selling oils, we are each reminded that healing is not an event, but rather a journey we walk as we make our way back to the memory of God. Love is the not-so-secret ingredient in every bottle. Each blend is stirred with prayers for healing. Val, who worked for two years as the head of our shipping department before taking a better job, always said a prayer for the givers and receivers of the oils after each bottle was ready to be shipped. Val, like every employee of Thistle Farms, began every morning in the meditation circle before she began to work. She said during her time at Thistle Farms she learned that surrender is quiet. She says in order for her to heal and forgive, she has to surrender everything. Through the journey of surrender, she learned how much quieter it was than all the fighting in prison, with family, and with the world. She comes from a horrific history that goes back further than she remembers, and she says she's still dealing with the ripple effects decades later. She knows that the women of Magdalene are not instantly healed, but are in a process of healing, and that in the midst of that we can still pray and work for others to do the same. I had the pleasure of being with Val when she first saw the ocean. As she stepped onto the beach, she took her shoes off and reached out to grab my hand. Then she immediately sat down and started calling her children to tell them their momma was on the beach. She was excited to see the ocean, but she was even more excited to share the news that she was seeing the ocean with her children.

Early memories of Mr. Price offering homemade healing recipes always felt like treasured knowledge that gave me some power in being able to participate in my own healing. The idea of creating recipes and concoctions to ease pain, clear our minds, stop infection, help us digest, clear sinuses, and help us deal with hundreds of other things that make us feel sick seemed like a great idea. The idea of mixing arts and crafts with justice and healing was exciting. What I didn't anticipate when this started was how much more these recipes and this business would offer.

The business of Thistle Farms has enabled conversations in almost every state and a growing number of countries about why women walk the streets and what's required for them to leave the streets. The balms, lotions, and oils offer a platform in faith communities, Rotary clubs, and spas about the reality of child sexual abuse and addiction. Beyond that, the products also offer hope, a means of prayer, and a path into the more mystical elements of faith and healing.

I'm constantly amazed at how our products open up bigger conversations. Just before I gave the keynote speech at a Lutheran pastors' conference in Ohio, an older man who was the pastor to a farming community approached me at the booth. Three women from Thistle Farms were working hard to unpack all our products. The scent of lavender balms and tea tree soaps drew people toward our booth.

This older pastor didn't appear to have any sense of humor or poetry. He took one look at our I'M A THISTLE FARMER bumper sticker and said something under his breath about how it was stupid. His response didn't surprise any of us. In general, people are skeptical about our name and our claim that we create beautiful products and wrap them in paper made from a noxious weed. For farming communities, the thistle weed has been the bane of their existence. They've spent days wanting to be anywhere but in the field digging up the deepest taproot on the planet. It is alarming for some when we waltz in and set up a booth that praises thistles for being beautiful and healing.

"Do you not think we understand?" I asked him. "We know what the thistle is, and that's how some women have been treated in this world. That's the point."

The man and one of his colleagues sent us a box after the event. When we opened the package, we found hundreds of thistles they'd harvested. We used them to create our handmade thistle cards. It was a beautiful gift.

Not too long ago I visited my sister Sandy, who lives in the house where we grew up. After my mom's death in 1997, she purchased the home, dumped all the contact-papered appliances, remodeled, and landscaped the property. One day when I went to visit, I walked around the cul-de-sac that dead ends right at Mr. Price's house. It's a walk that brings me full circle. Each house holds a story, and when I walk, my old memories jump out and walk alongside me. I smell, hear, and see myself at that tender age again as I walk by the willow and maple that were my first companions. I walk by old shortcuts that shaved maybe a minute or two off my sprints back home.

As I approached Mr. Price's home his son pulled up in a mint-condition truck—the apple doesn't fall far from the tree. He told me his dad had died a few months before. I told him how sorry I was, and that his father was a great man. I wanted to tell him that I can still smell his pipe when I walk around and that I can still taste the mayo and bologna sandwiches on Wonder bread he would carry out under the peach tree on Saturdays. As his son pulled away I wanted to tell him I was going to miss the person who was the healing balm to my childhood.

One of the sweetest memories of Mr. Price that I carry with me is that he could fill a whole afternoon with a peach. He taught me that a peach is good for many purposes. You can eat peaches, carve the pits, burn the wood, compost the leftovers, sit in the shade, study the worms, and talk about the memory of last year's peaches and next year's harvest possibilities. I can still feel the itch above my lip from sitting and eating fuzzy peaches and listening to Mr. Price explain the ways of the world. He made the most common yards seem full of possibility and magic. He taught me that nature herself is a healer at heart. He knew the birds of the sky and the grass of the field and considered them worthy of his time and reflection. He never preached but taught me more about truth than just about any preacher.

I doubt Mr. Price ever expected to be the first of many casual gurus who practiced the art of healing using practical things with a spiritual lightness. He was fun and without even trying to be too teacherlike. He offered me a healing balm I can still take out and use to soothe my weary soul. He still serves as a beacon for me when the weight of what I am carrying seems a bit heavy. When I close my eyes, I can see him standing in his driveway contemplating peach trees and crabgrass and drawing on his pipe, and a sweet peace fills the space between now and then. He made the yoke easier and the burden lighter, and inspired me to do the same for others.

Chapter Four

THROUGH THE HARD, DRY GROUND

Lavender Blend

2 ounces aloe vera oil
1 ounce olive oil
18 drops lavender essential oil
12 drops myrrh essential oil

In all of these recipes, I have tried to keep the ratio of essential oils to carrier oils about 10 drops to each ounce. You may like them a bit weaker or stronger; you will discover your preference as you go. For this recipe, pour the ingredients into a glass container and whisk to combine.

Lavender has been used for centuries to calm babies, and to heal wounds and burns. Myrrh combined with lavender creates a blend

that is renowned for its calming influence,
and when combined with geranium, the blend
is helpful as an antiseptic for minor cuts and
skin problems. This lavender blend is one of
my favorites for any areas of cracked skin.
The oil moisturizes the skin, brings healing,
and offers peace.

THE APPLE PIE CARRIES as rich a history as casseroles and snake oils in our national identity. The early 1970s was a time when microwaves and garbage disposals were still considered fancy or "newfangled." One of the best examples of when good old love and natural remedies lost their place completely on the American shelf was the advent of the mock apple pie. The recipe for mock apple pie appeared on the back of the Ritz cracker box sometime around that same time and described how you could make apple pie without using apples. The irony that the only good things in apple pie are the apples was lost on us who were amazed that, quickly and cheaply, we could get the same taste. My mom made them, and we devoured them. We consumed an empty-calories concoction of sugar and butter with Ritz crackers in a pie shell. And I loved the sugary sweetness so much I don't think I missed the apples at all. Never mind that the food wasn't healthy or that crackers replaced the one decent ingredient in the dessert. We simply loved that it was new and quick and easy to make.[1]

Most people want healing to be like the mock apple

pie—quick, painless, and easy. We aren't interested in learning about the old ways of making tinctures or teas. Really, not much has changed. We still want someone to cast a prayer like a spell so we can throw down our crutches. We want to get diagnosed and then swallow a pill to make the pain go away. We're willing to buy the pitch from the latest guru who promises that if we take the right medicine or believe the right way—and if God is in a good mood—we will be cured. Sometimes we're left wondering if we didn't get the prayer right, or if all oils are just a bunch of empty promises. In that environment, we are sold a raw deal, end up feeling cynical, or lump the rich history of the art of healing and oils into our worst notion of what it means to sell snake oils.

Our desire for quick and easy doesn't slip into just the notion of healing if we aren't careful and can become part of every area of our life. I know, because I've been guilty of it myself.

By the time I went to seminary, I knew I wanted real apples in my pie. I had learned to love the woods and had read books on the subject, including *Where the Lilies Bloom* and *Walden*. I wasn't sure what my vocation as a priest would look like, but I knew that I wanted to live deeply in the truth that love heals. I didn't see myself as a parish priest, but instead dreamed of working in Africa or starting a program for women. When I met my husband, his father was the director of USAID, the United States Agency for International Development in Botswana. We spent one summer in divinity school working in Botswana with his family. The experience was life-changing in its breadth and depth with a thousand new shades of color to take in. During these years I was learning from teachers, literature, and experience the gifts inherent in the coneflowers, rosemary, and lavender all blooming around me. I felt pretty certain that life wasn't fair and that poverty was a human construction. We both invent and tolerate poverty. In seminary, I began wrestling more in depth with how faith takes into account the pain we inflict upon each other. I began discovering more about the long tradition of healers, saints, and prophets who understood that the suffering of others was an integral part of our relationship with God.

One of the great teachers and theologians I read about was Howard Thurman. He was an African American raised at the time Jim Crow was the law in the South. He was an advocate for universalism, met with Gandhi, influenced Martin Luther King Jr., and served as a chaplain at Boston University. One thing that stood out for me was a story he told about when he was a child. He was wearied by the world and went out to the woods to find solace. He talked about the relationship he felt to a big oak tree and how he could sit under the tree and feel healing. I loved that he was a mystic and a passionate activist. I met his wife while I was in divinity school and even got to interview her for a paper I was writing. I also loved reading about Dorothy Day and all the old saints who formed communities and combined economic justice into their ideals of vocation.

For me, faith that contained real apples had to be mature enough to face the question *Why is there suffering?* It's not a question with an answer. Seminary offered me the freedom to explore the question of suffering, the definitions of sin, and the similarities regarding suffering among different faith traditions. I began to understand that suffering is a deep condition experienced by all people because of our temporal nature and eternal longing. To take suffering seriously is to take the human experience seriously.

Suffering is like hard, dry ground. Though wholly a part of God's green earth, the seeds below the surface need tenacious strength and determination to push through and grow in parched land. Such hard, dry ground requires grace like water poured over it. It requires strong seeds that adapt to a harsher climate and a vision that can make the barren beautiful. An old prayer from a group of nuns in Singapore asks God to overturn the hard ground of our lives even though we weep. The prayer goes on to ask God to dig deep furrows and sow new seed that will grow freely. Suffering is hard ground, but it can become the richest soil through attention and nurturing. Suffering invites us to acknowledge the pain before us and pay attention to the needs in front of us.

It's hard to dig very deeply into the topic of suffering without running into the notion of sin. Yet all too often sin is used to point out the faults in others, rather than to free us from traps that prevent us from loving God. One of the best examples of this comes from a passage found in the Gospel of John. Jesus encounters a blind beggar. When the disciples see the blind man, they ask, "Who sinned, this man or his parents...?" Jesus' closest followers want to know, "Who's to blame?"

The questioning implies that if the blind beggar is a sinner, then we don't have a responsibility to help because the suffering he endures is deserved. Jesus uses the question as an opportunity to teach that culpability—establishing guilt or responsibility for sin—is the not the main issue whenever we encounter suffering in the world. The issue of culpability simply lies in our response to suffering and our ability to love with compassion, not judgment.

The Gospel of John also tells us that Jesus, with nothing but spit and dirt, makes a healing and soothing mud for the man. This beautiful, simple, and earthy action preaches that redemption is possible, even when we feel incapable of addressing the suffering we meet along the way. The whole story breathes life into the old theology of blame and exclusion and invites us to respond in love and inclusiveness.

Job is another character from the Bible who exemplifies the depth and meaning of suffering with grace. In Job's story, a just man endures the worst kind of suffering possible: his children die. His friends try to justify the suffering by defending God in the face of this grief. The arguments are hollow. Job dismisses them. He makes a final plea to the creator and demands an explanation. By the end of the story, God speaks to him out of a whirlwind and asks him where he was when the earth was formed. He asks Job if he can make a sunrise or move a mountain. In the conversation, God doesn't give an answer. He does, however, reveal his presence. Job teaches us that suffering creates a theological crisis between us and the meaning of life. When we undergo pain we seek mercy, not justice, from our creator. Job teaches us that it is in that suffering that we meet God.

Not too long ago I was called to the hospital to pray for a beautiful little girl named Keesha, the daughter of Jordan, one of the manufacturing directors of Thistle Farms. The ordeal at the hospital lasted about twenty-four hours, and it left me reeling in the wake of that tidal wave of suffering. I left the hospital as her family and close friends said goodbye to Keesha. For almost a day she was kept alive on a respirator. Her hair was still in neat cornrows with shiny clear beads that looked like prisms. We offered prayers and anointed her with oil. The family wept and held on to each other as Psalms 139 and 23 were read. She was pronounced dead at 2:57 p.m. Jordan called to say that even though her baby girl died, she would be on a ventilator for another day to ensure Keesha's organs could be donated. The conversation with Jordan was overwhelmingly generous and yet so deeply sad. The experience made me want to wave a white flag and surrender. Jordan is an orphan from Brazil who says she lived through times where she was treated worse than a dog. A couple from the United States adopted her when she was seven, but she was on the streets by the time she was sixteen. When she got pregnant at nineteen, she called the baby her light. She got clean and sober and never prostituted or did drugs again. She and her sweet daughter shared the same birthday. They were exactly twenty years apart.

When I left the hospital, Jordan was draped over the bed—too exhausted to grieve standing up. And now she was offering the child's organs to others in need. The act of generosity demonstrates bravery beyond anything I've seen. I know she knows about loss and pain. I know she knows about how love heals. It makes me weep to imagine her lifting her head off the bed and saying, "Yes, you can take my precious child's organs." It makes me want to be grateful for everything and love everyone with gentleness. It makes me want to take a wide turn around theology and stay close to the ground. Sometimes nothing is left to say when suffering has made it impossible to stand.

The suffering of the innocent in the world is not a question to be answered but a space of deep relationship, where God comes out of the whirlwind and you are with God, addressing the deepest issues of life itself. Often God will remind us of our place in that creation. Without some sense of meeting God in that suffering, it is almost too much to bear. So we find places to encounter God in that suffering.

When we hear the story of Jesus healing the blind man, Job, or Jordan's story, suffering humbles us and reminds us of all the mud, and casseroles, and compassion people have given us. We can't help but live in gratitude and express that gratitude by loving others the way we have been loved, without judgment and without blame. While there may never be an adequate answer to the question of why there's suffering in the world, faith asks us to engage the question deeply and with our whole hearts.

Suffering and healing don't always take place in

consecutive moments. I didn't suffer in elementary school and then heal in seminary. The movement toward healing comes in small waves, cloudy visions, and rambling paths. Dancing between suffering and healing can come in moments I breathe in deeply or allow tears to flow freely.

I remember sitting under a dogwood tree one spring day in seminary. The tree was unusual in that the flowers were half pink and half white. Someone had grafted branches together and the tree grew into a beautiful anomaly. This grafted tree whose growth seemed impossible gave me the hope that healing could take root in me. The place in the trunk where the grafting took place had grown into a small burly knot, a tree's version of scarring. That struck me as beautiful. The places of brokenness and scars can become the most valuable and beautiful. Woodworkers who turn wood to make candlesticks, bowls, and railings search for burly knots to make the most beautiful bowls. The place of the scarring creates character in the rings within the wood and unfurls in unique patterns. It was while I was taking a class that described the idea of redemptive suffering that I went and sat under that tree. I reflected on all the people who showed me through their loving actions and words that the suffering I had known as a child could be redeemed—that it could be the source of healing and compassion. I thought about my first dance teacher, who saw something graceful in me. I thought about the resident assistant in my dorm at Sewanee who came into my room once while I was crying. She encouraged me to apply for an internship that expanded my horizons and gave me a broader vision. Marcus, who I met in divinity school and later married, sat with me under that tree regularly that first spring as we dreamed about our life together. That half pink and half white dogwood, among all the ivory towers at Vanderbilt University, was my hallowed ground where I could sit and think. The tree still blooms in front of the seminary, and every March as the blossoms unfold I make my pilgrimage to bathe in its brilliant pink and white dappled light.

During my three years of divinity school signs emerged that I was moving from a wounded heart toward something stronger. As I was making my way through the ordination process I didn't hesitate to voice what I believed when I sat in front of the committee that determined if I would become ordained. Without fear of reprisal I spoke of my belief in the universal love of God for the whole world. When they asked about my theology, I spoke from my heart and with the knowledge I had soaked in from theologians such as F. D. Maurice, Albert Schweitzer, and Martin Luther King Jr. These leaders were fearless, and I wanted to learn to speak with clarity about the fields of justice. Another sign of healing was when that old church where my father worked and where I was molested was razed to the ground. It was then rebuilt into a parking lot for a grocery store. The change made it possible for me to drive down that road. Instead of visiting old ghosts, I could buy fresh food and celebrate new life.

In some spaces of suffering, the pain eases. Those

spaces allow us to breathe for a minute or an hour and have enough energy to face the next wave of suffering coming our way. I have sat for years in meetings at Magdalene hearing such painful stories that I think there's no way through this. On top of the personal suffering that always comes with sexual violence, most of the women I have worked with have seemingly insurmountable court fines, long arrest records, and a trail of broken relationships. But almost always, as we leave a meeting, we get a break as someone says something funny or invites others to grab a bite of food or go out on the porch for a smoke. It's like we need breaks from thinking about it all and to let our minds and bodies rest. The remnants of suffering can last a long time, so it's important to take the road slowly.

After graduating from Vanderbilt Divinity School, I still had to complete one year of Anglican studies at St. Luke's Seminary, where I found inspiration in a mentor named Dr. Jack Gessell. Jack was a great teacher since I wanted to learn church history and how successful communities were formed. He was radical and opinionated. Fussy about theology, he loved the rituals and idea of church, and he spent his life prodding the communities he served to be more open and healing.

At the time, Marcus and I also discovered we were going to have a baby. We couldn't imagine how we were going to do it since he had a music publishing deal and was living in Nashville, and I was living back in Sewanee, Tennessee, for the year. We didn't have a home of our own but were living with family and friends. I was almost nine months pregnant when I was finally ordained and moved back to Nashville. In the Anglican rite of ordination, the ordinand kneels within a circle of priests who lay hands on the ordinand's head and shoulders. For me that meant that several of the priests who knew my father blessed my ordination. Ironically, my father, for all his beautiful thoughts, died thinking that women's ordination would be the end of the church.

I remember opening my eyes while I was on my knees as they sang and poured out their blessing. As I kneeled all I could see was tasseled black shoes. I knew in that moment that I was not going to be able to walk in their shoes. I wanted to travel on the hard, dry ground, and I needed shoes more appropriate for the journey I was making. I couldn't ever walk in my father's shoes.

Over the years my clothes and shoes haven't changed much. A few women who entered Magdalene have talked about being worried at first that a priest started the program. Clemmie, a funny and powerful speaker who came into Magdalene in 2004, and who has moved to New Orleans to help them begin a sister program, often recounts her image of me before she met me. She thought I was going to be in a "nun's outfit." She said she walked in and I had on some kind of "Daisy Duke" shorts and a T-shirt and she didn't think I could be a minister because my shoes were "all worn out and tired."

Even after ordination, I lacked the leadership qualities to start an organization and needed to learn how to raise money. Without a doubt, my image of leading a community came from my mom. She taught me to put money into programs before buildings and never to let it get you down. The "it" she was referring to changed. Sometimes "it" was needy volunteers who really needed her more than they wanted to give to her organization. Sometimes "it" was the bastards who set up such an unjust system that would mean she could never get ahead. Sometimes "it" was the enormous scope of the work and the fact that you are never, ever done. No matter what, don't let it get you down.

She demonstrated this one morning at about five a.m. when she called me and said, "St. Luke's is burning." St. Luke's was the community center where she began working as a childcare giver after my father died. She ended up being the executive director there for almost twenty years. I jumped in the car and met her out front with several fire trucks whose pulsing lights filled the predawn sky. All the offices and part of the old library were gone. The rest of the library smoldered. Just as the fire seemed contained, she wiped her eyes, pulled out a pad and pen, and began making a to-do list. Using the light from the fire trucks so she could see to write, she began to rebuild even before the smoke cleared from the fire.

When after seminary I started working downtown with men and women who were homeless, I met a Catholic priest named Charlie Strobel. He had opened a shelter for the homeless, and I spent hours down there volunteering and memorizing all the stories he would share about how he came to this work. It fascinated me that he too had lost his father at a young age and had a strong and compassionate mother. He had a great sense of humor, although sometimes a bit dark. He still played baseball in what one of his friends called "an under one hundred league." I loved having a friend who wanted to serve God by loving people and who interpreted his faith through the lens of compassion. He had his own story that informed his ministry and shaped how he treated the men and women who came into his center. One of the things I admired most about him was his honesty and candor in his faith. He was open about all his doubts and frustrations and never pretended that because he was faithful, everything was going to be fine. He has continued to help me as I have tried to carve my own path. Charlie taught me that you could be cynical about some of the church dogma and give a wide berth to institutions, but you have to get close to suffering if you want to serve people who are homeless or imprisoned.

I used to wonder if I could ever complain about the suffering I have known in my own life given that it pales in comparison to others' suffering. Every time I struggled I would think, *Well, I'm not a refugee from war,* or *I don't have it as bad as so and so.* Now I try to honor the suffering I have known and respect the suffering of others. I try to remember that when I encounter the suffering of others, I am encountering God. A few years ago I took a trip to Rwanda to help a women's social enterprise. One day a young man led us on a tour of a church where several thousand people were slaughtered. On the wall were stacks of bones. Blankets, bottles, and shoes from the children killed were displayed on another wall. The tour guide explained that he lost his whole family. All of us on the trip were crying, but a part of me wondered if I had a right to cry. Where was I when the genocide in Rwanda was taking place in 1994?

Yet I knew I wouldn't be human if I didn't cry at the sight of such suffering. I wouldn't be a person who wants to be healed and wants to heal others if I didn't weep in the face of some of the worst suffering this world has known. After the tour, we stood on the hard ground outside the church. I thought about all the suffering and the wounds we inflict upon one another. I thought about the way the universal truths of suffering are endured by individuals. I thought about people who try to help ease the suffering of others on grand and small scales. There were huge, old pine trees around the property, standing straight and tall. The trees that witnessed the atrocity kept growing through this old, hard ground. Healing has to be like those trees, able to push through the ground, bear witness, and keep growing.

By early 1995, I had been ordained for several years, but I was still just dreaming of creating a small community. I was at the critical juncture between dreaming and making something come to life. To make it actually real seemed like too much. I was trying to raise a child and was pregnant with my second son. My husband was on the road trying to make it as a country singer. He had a deal with Columbia Records and had just released the single "Honky Tonk Mona Lisa." The record company had decided that for him to make it on radio he should go visit every country radio station in the United States of America. I was working four days a week in the downtown area in addition to working as a chaplain at St. Augustine's Chapel at Vanderbilt, and I was exhausted. It occurred to me that it might be impossible to create this home for women, work as a chaplain, and be a good wife and involved mom.

I was getting ready to head home from my work downtown with my son in tow one day when it all changed. As I was leaving the office and making my way toward the car, I wondered if I should put the idea of starting a community for women on hold for another year or so. The dream was wonderful, but the reality of living it didn't seem like a great idea when I started thinking about how much work it would take to make it happen. These are the moments when we kill many of our dreams. It's sad to think that some of our sweetest dreams die when we can't imagine them coming true and we choose to let them fade silently into the bright light of day. When we got to the car my son decided he didn't want to get into his car seat and began to arch his back. I was trying to get him to sit still long enough for me to get the seat belt around him when he asked me, "Mom, why is that lady smiling?"

I looked up and realized he had seen the enormous sign dangling in front of the Classic Cat, a strip club that boasted exotic dancers and topless waitresses. The sign showed a smiling woman in a string bikini with cat ears and a tail. My heart raced and then sank. *What do I tell him?* I wondered. Would I tell my son that it is just how the world is, and some people get paid for dressing up like cats? Would I tell him that some people use each other for their own gain? Would I tell him it's close to Halloween and not to worry? I decided to tell him that some people don't respect other people, especially women.

I remember two feelings as I stared at the sign. One was a kind of sadness for my son's short-lived innocence in this world. At the innocent age of four, the sight of a grown woman dressed up like a cat seemed ridiculous and comical to him. Before long such an image would fade into his cultural understanding of women. Soon this sign would blend into a larger cultural picture, where it's not uncommon in malls, on billboards, and in magazines to see images of women who look like they are willing to be bought and sold like cats. Later he would learn that we even designate some women as prostitutes and sell them for less than pets. The other thought was a rush of new conviction for the work that we were beginning. I knew the road ahead meant confronting all kinds of barriers, which would be hard, but I wanted to be the kind of person who acts on her beliefs and tries to be a part of healing.

The women I've met over the past fifteen or so years, many of whom had to dress up like cats or in other ridiculous outfits, opened my eyes to the abuse and daily fears of being bought and sold. Sharing stories and reflecting on times when the women of Magdalene were willing to dress up in costumes and smile helps us all realize how far we have traveled.

I met a remarkable woman about five years ago. She

danced at the Classic Cat when she was seventeen years old. Long before she came to the big city of Nashville to dance, she suffered plenty in the rural hills of Tennessee. She was abused, beaten, and scared. She believed something must be wrong with her to be the target of so much anger and abuse. Somehow she didn't get the message that all children should hear: *You are priceless.*

Soon after she arrived in Nashville, she began working with a pimp. Her life turned into a nightmare for the next twelve years. She ended up in a prison for two years. A friend of hers told her about Magdalene. She came to be an important part of the community. She spent almost a year working at Thistle Farms, and it seemed like she was a living example that even though you were bought and sold for less than the price of some pets, you can still fill a community with joy in your presence. I heard her retelling her story once, and she sobbed as she described her gratitude for finding this community. She said she could not have imagined this life back in the days of the Classic Cat.

Tragically, she ended up in a very bad relationship that led to her return to prostitution and drugs. The damage done to people when you buy, abuse, and sell them continues to take its toll on them. She lived clean and sober for almost two years, but she ended up back on the streets and back in prison. She has no idea of her beauty, worth, and belovedness, and until she does, she will continue to sell herself so short that she is left with nothing. I didn't know who she was when I started Magdalene, or who any of the hundreds of women who have graced the doorway were. It was a smiling but nameless woman dressed in a cat suit who gave me the impetus to start the wheels turning. Developing this community is an effort to stake a claim in the events and circumstances in our community, and try to help make it better, especially for our children.

One of my favorite aspects of the work I do with the women of Magdalene is spending time on the road with the graduates of the community. We'll travel together to speak somewhere, sell our oils and salves, and hear horrific and hilarious stories of life on the streets. I heard a story years ago from a graduate of Magdalene who had danced in a club. She said every night she had to do a "jungle dance" and move about on the pole with a live python around her. She laughed and laughed telling the story, but then she gave a heavy sigh and said, "I don't know how I did it."

Not too long ago a group of three Magdalene graduates and I traveled to Iowa to speak at a Lutheran university. About ten minutes before the convocation began we stood outside preparing for the session. We discussed what message would be best to share with the college students to inspire them. One of the women spoke up. She said she could tell them about the time she couldn't turn another trick because the crack house she lived in was infested with mosquitoes. She said the only thing she could do to stop getting bitten was walk outside and get arrested. We all laughed together at the description of the scene. The thought that being covered in mosquito bites could be the beginning of healing is crazy, sad, and yet funny.

My son's question about the smiling lady dressed up

like a cat was the answer to the call to learn what it means to be a healer. We organized a board within a year and several of us organized a group from the city of Nashville to create a task force to think about how we could have a positive impact. I started meeting kind souls who gave money, and gifted volunteers like Jane, Cary, Jeff, Rosemary, John, Linda, Gilbert, Rod, Rick, Dick, Bobby, Charlie, Toni, Michael, Sandy, and many others who helped share the work and brought their needed gifts. I established relationships with the women I wanted to serve. Sometimes it's images like the lady in the cat suit that push us through the hard, dry ground.

Chapter Five

THE SEARCH FOR GILEAD

An Anointing Oil

3 ounces olive oil
1 teaspoon 100 percent shea butter
10 drops rose essential oil
5 drops bergomot essential oil
10 drops grapefruit essential oil

This recipe introduces shea butter into the
mix to give the mixture viscosity while also
promoting soft skin. Combine the olive oil
and the shea butter in a pan over low heat
until the shea butter has completely melted.
Remove from heat, pour into a plastic
container, add the essential oils, and stir to
combine. This mixture creates a unique and
balanced blend. Stir it toward your heart,

and offer prayers for the people you want to share these oils with. Offer the oil as a gift, or anoint the person you made it for on the feet or hands if the person is willing.

THE FIRST TIME I applied what I think of as snake oil to my body, in the broadest sense of the word, was to get a good base tan. A friend taught me to mix baby oil and iodine to magnify the sun's rays and make my skin turn darker faster. In my neighborhood, getting a tan was a goal that drove us to rooftops and blacktops as soon as we got out of school for the summer. More dedicated friends used other home potions like coconut milk with oil, transmission fluid, or olive oil with lemon juice. We poured lemon juice into our hair with hopes of highlights. I remember my mom being frustrated that we would squeeze entire bottles of reconstituted lemon juice on our hair, leaving her with none when she needed it for baking.

It never occurred to me when I was a teenager that the mixing of iodine and baby oil was the beginning of my journey in making snake oil, or that we were learning an ancient practice called anointing.

I was stumbling onto the path, unaware that I was following searchers from every generation that had come before. It was a sweet blend of chance and providence leading toward a longing for a balm that could heal. I was beginning to search for the balm of Gilead. Thinking back over those summers when we rubbed each other's back with oil and iodine to get a tan, I realize that we never considered the idea that slathering our bodies in oils was a practice older than Moses himself. The ingredients and intention may have been different, but we were the descendants of pilgrims searching for an Eden called Gilead.

Genesis introduces us to a place called Gilead. You can't find Gilead on a map, but the site lies somewhere east in the mountainous region of the kingdom of Jordan. The author of Psalm 60 writes of people suffering and having to taste wine that makes them reel. God responds to the people in their suffering by saying, "Gilead is mine."[1] Later other psalmists and poets describe Gilead as a balm and a place of healing and comfort. I believe it's more of an idea, like Eden, than a geographic location. Gilead represents the place that holds the hope of healing. For everyone who has been wounded, hurt, or abused, Gilead represents that sacred place where borders fade and balms are poured out lavishly. Gilead isn't a dream, but a place we find in our journeys toward healing. When we arrive, we look back and feel like we were walking toward it all along.

We are all descendants of Moses, a great Old Testament prophet and pilgrim who spent forty years in the wilderness searching for a Promised Land whose territory flowed with milk and honey. The book of Exodus describes how Moses, during the long search for a lush land, ventured up Mount Sinai and talked with God. Each time, Moses would come down the mountain with a word from God to share, a glow over his face, and—in the thirtieth chapter—a recipe for how to make healing oils. The story goes that Moses clung to a cleft between the rocks so that he could glimpse the back of God's head. That is the closest anyone in the history of our faith has come to seeing the face of God. All the other times up on that sacred mountain, Moses simply heard God's voice. Moses heard God in the mountains tell him: "Take the finest spices: of liquid myrrh five hundred shekels, and of sweet-smelling cinnamon half as much, that is, two hundred fifty, and two hundred fifty of aromatic cane, and five hundred of cassia—measured by the sanctuary shekel—and a hin of olive oil; and you shall make of these a sacred anointing oil blended as by the perfumer; it shall be a holy anointing oil."[2] Moses received a recipe for oils to help him lead the people toward wholeness, and the people listened.

The Bible contains hundreds of references to anointing with oils. Many more appear in the holy writs of every faith tradition. For shamans, rabbis, priests, and other healers, oils were part of sacred tool kits by which healing was instilled in the life of the faith community. The faithful poured oil on heads, feet, and hands, to celebrate, to set apart, and to heal. They even put oils on their loved ones when they died, to purify their bodies.

Anointing is a sacred and all-too-often lost practice. One of the most intimate moments in the Bible happens in the story of Nicodemus, who is mentioned only three times in the Gospel narrative yet plays a powerful role. At the beginning of John's Gospel, Nicodemus comes in the middle of the night to speak to Jesus about new life. Later, Nicodemus defends Jesus in front of the Sanhedrin after Jesus preaches in the temple. In his last appearance, Nicodemus asks for the body of Jesus after the crucifixion, and carries with him a mixture of myrrh and aloes, weighing about a hundred pounds. Nicodemus takes the body of Jesus in order to anoint the corpse with spices and oils before wrapping the body in linen cloths, according to traditional Jewish burial customs. The image of a religious man taking the broken and naked body of another and anointing it is both tender and powerful.

While using oils was a common practice, who performed the anointing and who was anointed adds significance. Anointing calls us to humility in our practice. Pouring oil on the newly dead people we have loved and tended is hard. The task is enormous and filled with lovingkindness. The eternal becomes closer when we touch the temporal with sacred oils.

For most ministers in mainline churches who use oils, the practice of anointing consists of the minister, with a prayer, placing a drop of consecrated oil in the sign of a cross on the forehead of someone who is sick or at the point of death. The act is both symbolic and sacramental. The oils are used symbolically to remind us of God's healing and presence. The oils are sacramental. They are an outward and visible sign of the inward and spiritual healing power of love. When we limit the use of oils to only this symbolic and sacramental way, I think we lose some of the real beauty and depth of the practice of healing with oils. We fail to acknowledge that the oils themselves can contain healing properties. Because the oils are powerful and medicinal, using them on heads, hands, and feet is healing for the person who is sick. Placing a generous amount of oil on the skin allows it to sink in and helps to restore the recipient's equilibrium and peace of mind. We have also forgotten that touching another body is a sacred act in itself.

When we use only a drop of oil, we lose the gift of filling a room with the fragrance of myrrh and aloe. In the church, I believe we need to use healing oils lavishly—anointing moms and dads, babies, sick people, and people being prepared for a special task. It is simply a matter of reclaiming a gift of creation that is a beautiful tradition.

In the earlier days of my priesthood I wanted to go back to the old Christian tradition of anointing babies with oil as a blessing during baptism, because baptism is the first sacrament of a community. I wanted to baptize similarly to the traditions in the Eastern Orthodox Church. When they baptize a baby the use of oils is a key ingredient to the ceremony. The baby is undressed and wrapped in a white towel as the priest blesses the water in the baptismal font. Then the priest adds olive oil that has been brought by the godparents and consecrated, and the baby is immersed three times. This anointing is a lavish display of the love poured out on us, and the practice harkens back to the anointing of kings and belief in the priesthood of all believers. In the pouring out of the oil, the child is sealed as Christ's own forever.

Because I had pondered this and decided I wanted to

baptize babies this way, when a friend I'd studied theology with called me and asked me to baptize her baby girl, I told her I was interested in using oils and adapting the old Eastern Orthodox tradition. We held the baptism at her home, and everyone present wrote a blessing and anointed a part of the baby's body with sweet olive oil. The baby's grandparents and cousins placed oil on her arms and legs and hair along with kisses and silent prayers. The ceremony was beautiful until the moment I tried to hold the baby in my arms to pour the water over her head. We'd unintentionally created a Slip'N Slide of an infant. I wrapped the child against my vestments so she wouldn't slide out of my arms. Since then I have refined the tradition so that we just anoint hands, head, and feet. Learning how to make and use oils is a lifelong quest.

The quest takes us back in time and beckons us to search the world for understanding. There is no place better in the world for me to remember the ancient traditions of healing, and my own ignorance, than central Africa. Many people there still practice the creative and old ways of living. Driving through the Masai Mara Reserve one summer, I discovered, tucked under the dashboard of the rental car, a book that described the healing properties of plants in Africa. After I hit a large pothole, the book came into view on the floorboard. I started leafing through *Medicinal Plants of the World* and couldn't believe the world of information I didn't know. The plant used to kill Socrates could be found nearby. A frankincense tree could grow in this hot climate and was used historically in temples and sacred spaces to disinfect the air in large crowds. I read about the marigold, that old common annual that I have seen all my life and not paid much attention to, that helps headaches and toothaches. I read about the Moringa tree, also called the miracle tree or mother's best friend in East Africa. Literally every part of the tree is used for healing: the pods, the bark, the leaves, and the flowers. If we want to be good healers, we are committing ourselves to lifelong learning and remain open to the unexpected gifts we find along the way.

Gilead too is truly a journey, not a destination, and as we travel toward that Promised Land it's good to remember that anyone—not just Moses and the Israelites—can get lost in the wilderness. We must be careful and tenacious as we make our way toward healing. It is a responsibility, and it can often be misused or misrepresented.

When Thistle Farms first started delving into healing oils years ago, I thought making the oils and distributing them would be fairly easy. But as we started to think about which oils to make, I realized that the sheer number of essential oil and blends to choose from would make it harder than anticipated. We decided to start with the oldest recipe we knew, the recipe that Moses received on Mount Sinai. We were all very excited that we were making the story our own. Three of us used an old pot in a friend's kitchen. We felt courageous and slightly mischievous, as if we were playing around with something too holy for our novice hands. The recipe from Exodus was challenging on several fronts. The Biblical blend instructs us to take myrrh ("five hundred shekels"), cinnamon ("two hundred fifty shekels"), cassia ("five hundred shekels"), and olive oil ("a hin"). It took us a while to determine the meaning of a "shekel" and a "hin." We had to consult a few websites and study a book called *Healing Oils of the Bible*.

Our first two attempts produced a thick residue at the bottom of our stirring pot. The cheesecloth didn't completely filter the cinnamon. We didn't know you could use oil from the cinnamon leaf and not actually use cinnamon. We also didn't understand how long things should steep or how oils should be heated. We laughed as we tried to talk each other into using it first. "No, you first, I insist," we kept saying to each other. We slowly refined the recipe, and now it's one the most popular products offered at Thistle Farms. Whenever I catch a whiff of the blend, it feels like it's the smell of prayer itself. When I use this oil to anoint someone, I feel like I am carrying part of my heart with the oils.

Some days, I want to take something as beautiful and mysterious as the balm of Gilead and anoint the women at Magdalene. I want to anoint the young, the old, and the recovering addicts—all women who long for healing.

One woman in particular stands out in my mind: Shana. Shana came to the Magdalene community almost two years ago. Her mom was an addict who thought she could use her daughter to persuade her dealer to give her drugs. One day, she sent Shana, then only thirteen years old, into the dealer's house in exchange for drugs. For the next ten years, she never left that home and worked for the dealer as a prostitute. Her mother had traded her for drugs. She was bought and sold a thousand times. I am not sure it's possible to imagine what she went through. Shana says the first person to shoot drugs into her was her mom, and that twice pimps sold her to other pimps. She says her tattoos are constant reminders of what she had to do on the streets to survive. She says she witnessed murder and was taken all over the country in an RV with other young women to make money for the people who "owned" her.

She came to Magdalene when her last pimp was arrested and sent to federal prison. She didn't know if she would stay, but she wanted to try a different life. Shana was scared because she didn't know how to live a life clean and sober and without hustling. Even though she has been with Magdalene for almost two years and with Thistle Farms as a sales associate for more than a year, she says that she still thinks it's a dream, that she's going to wake up and everything will disappear, as if Gilead is just wishful thinking. She is afraid that someone is going to make her go back to the hell of prostitution and addiction, or that she will be sent back to jail. As a community, we keep reassuring her that this way of living is real and that her old life is behind her.

During the Christmas rush—the most stressful season for everyone in retail—Shana stood up in the middle of the morning circle and did a cartwheel. She said she was happy to be busy and feel love at Christmastime. She expressed the joy of a child, fragile and contagious. I want to protect her and bottle that joy for harder days.

Whenever I see Shana, I'm tempted to reach for a bottle of our balm, pour oil over her feet, and keep her safe so that her healing can take root and she can remember who she is, beloved and worthy. Sometimes I feel afraid for her, that something will happen that she thinks she can't handle or that it will all just be too much. She embodies the truth that the ancient wounds of humanity are borne anew in every generation, and we have to help people heal in order to stop them from spreading into the next round of innocent children. We need to protect and anoint our children because they are holy. I pray she feels that she has stumbled into her own land of healing and keeps getting stronger.

One sign of her strength is that she is already reaching out to help new women coming into the community. She takes them for manicures and helps train them at Thistle Farms. That has always been a sign to me that people are healing, when they begin to reach out to another person and offer that person a hand. There are now "spa days" devoted to massaging the feet and hands of the newest residents. During those days volunteers and graduates use the balms we make with hot towels and massage. One of the graduates of the program, Julie, is a licensed massage therapist. She comes back every year and brings her massage chair. One by one, she offers the power of healing touch to her sisters who are just starting on the journey toward Gilead.

Anointing comes in many forms and fashions—the massages Julie offers on spa days, the laying on of hands by ministers visiting the sick, and the sweet cinnamon oils passed down for a thousand generations.

The hardest morning of the summer when we were working to open Magdalene was the day my mom woke up and couldn't walk or speak. No one anticipated that she would be dead six weeks later. We were scrambling for answers and couldn't believe that this woman who had raised a million dollars the year before to build a gymnasium for St. Luke's was no longer able to remember where she lived. This was also the same morning I woke up and thought I was having a miscarriage. I felt terrible as I wondered if I should go to the doctor for myself or go with my mom. I called my doctor, a close friend, who said I could come in for a quick checkup and then proceed to the hospital. The doctor examined me and told me there was no heartbeat and confirmed the miscarriage.

I hurried over to the hospital to be with my mom. A nurse who was reading my mom's chart while she was being wheeled into a room looked up at me and said, "Anne Stevens? Was she married to a priest named Joe Stevens?"

"Yes," I said, "but he died back in 1968." The nurse's question was like a comforting drink of hot tea after a long walk in a cold drizzle. Not one person in my whole adult life had ever asked me that question.

The nurse said, "It was my house where your father

stopped before he died. My mother and father were having a really hard time, and he spoke with them in our living room. I was just a child, but the story in our family is that he saved their marriage."

I don't know why it had never occurred to me or my siblings to ask about the house my father had visited, but the fact that thirty years later this stranger, on one of the strangest mornings of my life, was saying my father had saved her parents' marriage was completely overwhelming. There she was, a nurse, looking after my mother and loving her. I still had a miscarriage and my mother still eventually died, but I experienced healing because it didn't feel like my life was spinning out of control. Mercy and grace were standing in front of me, welcoming me to stay and be at peace.

It's all healing-the-crazy memories, the random encounters with nurses, and the humble beginnings of Magdalene. What they all hold in common is that they all occurred simultaneously in the summer of 1997. By that time, I had been ordained for six years and could feel the limitations of the tools and practices offered to me as a priest in the church. I was just feeling my way toward Gilead, and I needed to take some more deliberate steps. Other friends and colleagues also wanted to figure out more intentional and bigger steps that we could take together. The use of the oils was going to be a significant part of that journey. I knew in my heart I still longed subconsciously for Gilead. Like many before me, I longed for healing waters like a deer longs for a babbling brook. I wanted the healing waters laced with tonics and spices that would bring peace and depth to my prayer life. I want to use those oils my whole life, until they carry me through to the other side of time. When I am lying down to die, I want someone to recite the prayer in the Book of Common Prayer that says, "Go forth faithful servant," put some lavender oil on me, and then feel like they helped heal me. If I thought someone at my deathbed was praying for me to stand up and walk, I would hope someone else close by would invite that person into silence to remember that there is healing in death.

Over the past several years I've been trying to incorporate oils and anointing more into my daily life. With the help of gifted volunteers we have set up a table at my church with a variety of essential oils like lavender, cinnamon leaf, lemongrass, jasmine, champa, tuberose, geranium, balsam, and myrrh. Next to the oils, we have some empty bottles and note cards that explain the use of each essential oil. We invite people to make a blend of essential oils mixed with carrier oils like olive oil and jojoba oil and to carry them back with a prayer of love into their world, to be used on the hands and feet of the people they are serving. At first, the practice may seem contrived and somewhat awkward, but as people get used to the idea, they find themselves delighting in the process. Many return with stories of wonder and gratitude. I've even started offering the oils in settings like premarital counseling and blessings of pregnant women, and I have invited people to take the rest of the oils home.

People love using oils made especially for them. I often hear that people put homemade oils they receive from a friend in a special place so they won't get lost or misused. They see the oils as treasures, and the oils become part of their rituals, something they use before going to bed or when they wake up. I know couples preparing for marriage that use the oils once a week as prayer for each other as they prepare in body, mind, and spirit to stand at the altar and take their vows. One woman told me that she used the oils I gave her before every chemo treatment she received. She said she felt the healing of the treatments taking root since she felt more open to healing. The oils are especially appropriate as gifts in times of transition, when we often need new rituals and things to feel more rested and peaceful.

I've always anointed my three boys with my homemade balms. I'll mix a few essential oils with shea butter and olive oil from the kitchen. Then I massage the concoction into their feet and think about what a gift it is to be their mom. I anoint them in part because the oils are good for them. Natural snake oils increase our wellness and help boost our immune system. Rubbing their feet is good for their circulation and makes their feet look (and smell!) better. But it's more than that. When my oldest son comes home from college, within a few days he will ask me to use the balm on his feet. I am so grateful I still get to sow that kind of tenderness in my growing kids. I have tried to make anointing a ritualized part of every pilgrimage, retreat, circle, and worshipping community of which I am a part.

Other faith leaders have asked me to help them expand

their practice of anointing. Some time ago, I offered a weekend-long conference to a group of priests to show them how to make their own unique blends of oils. At the end of the conference we gathered all of the oils we had made, put them on the altar, and jointly offered prayers for healing. Since that conference I have received many emails telling me about experiences they have had with members of their community who felt cared for and loved in the presence of the oils.

More recently, I gave a keynote speech at a gathering of hospital chaplains and talked about how oils might be offered. There was a lot of resistance because of concerns about boundaries for chaplains and the requirements of different denominations. I respect those boundaries and the rules of various denominations and faith traditions. What I found good about the conference was that we eventually talked about the oils the chaplains wanted for their personal use and for friends and family. All the chaplains loved the stories and the oils, and learning how they could help their various ministries—even if they never brought a vial of oil into a hospital room.

I love that the process of anointing and oils helps me find my way to Gilead. I love that they are grounded in nature. Their very existence gives us permission to look more closely at our surroundings and see what healing treasures lie all around us. And the first signs of the path to healing may be closer than we think.

Chapter Six

HEALING COMES
AT A COST

Chamomile Balm

2 ounces sweet almond oil
8 drops frankincense essential oil
6 drops chamomile essential oil
6 drops lavender essential oil

Pour all of the ingredients into a glass jar and
whisk to combine. You may want to add a few
drops of your favorite essential oil in place of
the lavender, depending on the purpose of the
oil. Use this as a massage oil for the skin, or
add a capful to your bath. This peaceful and
restorative recipe helps reduce swelling. The
rich oil is cleansing for your feet, hands, and
arms. It is best used with your feet elevated,
or when you are in repose.

SNAKE OIL

I GREW UP LEARNING about the kinship between snake oil salesmen and faith healers from television. Back in the early years of television evangelists, my three sisters, my brother, and I filled hours and hours of our childhoods draped over the couch and sprawled out on the shag carpeting in the paneled den watching TV. Left to our own devices, we would lounge around for most of the day.

Some Saturdays we would lie around, sprawled out on the furniture with nothing but three channels to watch. Before the professional bowling show began, we would watch Ernest Angley while my mom baked homemade bread. He was an awesome and ridiculous faith healer who wore pastel suits with shiny lapels, perfectly folded kerchiefs, and a hairpiece that didn't quite match his hair. Thousands of people showed up for his revivals and lined up for him to touch them with his healing hands. He was a quintessential snake oil salesman in the worst sense of what that means. He sold people a dream with little regard for their actual pain. Watching him and the overly exaggerated way he would say "Gawd" and "Jee-sus," we wondered, *Who's buying this?* Nonetheless, we kept watching and giggling and imitating him by thumping each other on the head. The whole spectacle on the television was a strange joke to us, but I can imagine that it wasn't as funny to people in real pain, people who thought they weren't getting better because they lacked faith or got the prayer wrong. In my life, healing hasn't come free, nor has it come easily. There's always been a cost to healing. If the old adage "there is no free lunch" is true, then the corresponding truth is that there is no free healing either. Healing cannot happen without scars, and those scars cost us.

No matter where you are on your journey of healing, you always need to be careful about who you seek healing from. Just this past summer while traveling in Kenya to visit with a group of women who were beginning their own social enterprise, I pulled up behind a truck with about thirty people packed inside, many of whom looked very frail and sick. The travelers must have journeyed for many hours to see a healer in the nearby hills. They looked desperate. Their fear and misery was so raw, I couldn't help but add my own prayer. I prayed that the person they were looking for wouldn't claim things that were untrue, that the person wouldn't abuse them, and that in the exchange everyone might find some healing. I also prayed that the people in the back of the truck would find their way into some of the medical clinics that were scattered around the countryside.

I have learned a lot about faith healers from my gifted friend and pastor Russ Taff. A fine preacher in his own right, he's won several Grammys for his deep and spiritual voice. His daddy was an old-time Pentecostal preacher who held revivals, and he grew up traveling with him. Russ would sing while his dad shouted and prayed. Then he would invite people to come forward and put their feet in what he called the pool of Bethesda. The actual pool of Bethesda was described in the Bible as a miraculous place of healing. Russ and his dad didn't have much money, so they had to use a small dishpan as the pool at their tent revivals. This particular dishpan wasn't big enough for both feet so people who came down to the front of the tent for healing and repentance could only stick one foot at a time into the dishpan's tepid water. Russ offers a deep belly laugh as he recounts the story but also remembers that this unsuspecting holy place was where some pretty scared people found solace.

I have known people who have done quite a bit of damage in the name of God to folks with chronic diseases and paralysis. I went to hear Reid Ward at a poetry reading up on the Cumberland plateau in Tennessee. I sat on folding chairs with about sixty people in a common space on a campus and listened as Reid recited his poetry from his wheelchair; an accident had paralyzed him as a teenager. Without hors d'oeuvres, background music, microphones, flowers, or introductions, he began reading with stark honesty. He read with authority and vulnerability into a silent audience that was pulling for him in unified breaths.

Reid recited his poem "Faith Healers," about his experience when a young woman asked him if she could pray for him when he was at a local coffee shop. He read, "She put one hand on my head and the other on a paralyzed knee and said, 'Abba, Abba, Gibble Dee Gobble Dee Gew. Amen.'" The words provided a perfect poetic description of the arrogance of people who want to impose their faith on someone and the harm that can be inflicted on another. He read with a voice steeped in truth mixed with a kind of pain that opens the ears of the listeners to the reality, humiliation, awkwardness, and sadness of the scene. We sat in silence and could hear the truth for a minute in twisted, wise verse. Maybe that is the only way we can ever really hear it.

Maybe strangers who want to lay hands on you should simply buy you a cup of coffee and wish you a good day. There are folks who want to impose themselves upon people whose injured bodies have confused their matrix that maps out God's interaction with the world. To keep the matrix consistent, they need the innocent to stop suffering. In their arrogance, they think that if *they* pray the *right* prayers in the *right* way that God will be moved to finally get the paralyzed up and walking. They ignore the possibility that the individual and a hundred people who love that person have already offered prayers in the sweet silence of their hearts. They have a log in their eye so large that they cannot see that God is sitting there, right in front of them. I have come to think that everyone who wants to pray prayers of intercession—including myself—first needs to take a long bath in humility before saying word. I have heard too many stories from people who have had to get far away from religious people to find any sense of healing and peace. Reid is a remarkable teacher and poet whose daily journey should silence folks on a regular basis.

We must be vigilant and careful about whom we invite to be part of our healing journey. When we're sick or wounded, we're more susceptible to falling for a scam. Once we're tricked, we can easily become cynical about the hope of healing.

Shelia, Gwen, Jordan, Shana, Penny, Jennifer, Katrina, and Chelle are among many of the women who work at Thistle Farms who are experts at discerning a bad snake oil salesman from the real thing. They all talk about the survival skills of instant discernment that saved their lives more than once on the street.

Chelle, who has lived at Magdalene for two years, is a great mother to her children and keeps all the employees at Thistle Farms laughing. She is one of the most reliable employees I have ever had the opportunity work with. She always arrives early, can find absolutely anything in the entire manufacturing facility no matter how small, and will help you sort through any problem you have. When I asked her to explain how she managed to discern the difference between a good and a bad snake oil salesman on the streets, she simply said she trusted her gut. I kept thinking there had to be more. She said that in the instant you decide whether or not to get into the car with a stranger you have to trust your gut. Nothing else on the streets can keep you alive—there's no manual or guidebook.

"Trust your gut" doesn't seem like enough to go on for most people. But it was enough for Chelle to keep her alive on dangerous streets at the most dangerous hours of the night for more than twelve years. She didn't always get it right, and she paid an enormous price those times she got it wrong. But if you ask Chelle today, she says she still trusts her gut. It is her intuition that keeps her safe and on the path of recovery.

You can also tell a good snake oil salesman from a bad one by the salesman's claims. Whenever you read a claim that's too good to be true, rest assured that you're looking into the eyes of a snake. At a local health store recently there was a pamphlet on "healing" put out by an all-natural drug company. The brochure claimed the modern use of the term "aromatherapy" came from the French chemist René-Maurice Gattefossé in the 1930s. When this chemist suffered burns to his arm in a laboratory accident, he plunged his arm into a vat with lavender and the healing was miraculous. The booklet reports that despite suffering a third-degree burn, he made a quick recovery with no scars. When I read it in a pamphlet years later, his story makes it easy to see how quickly one can leap from healing oils to miraculous snake oils. A corrupt snake oil salesman tends to make huge claims about the wondrous properties of the oils.

The most honest approach to essential oils seems to be that there are healing properties in all-natural oils that are beneficial, and used over time with the right intention and methods, they can play an important role in the healing process. When that process includes the laying on of hands, massage, prayer, and meditation, the healing can be magnified, but there is no magic formula that will take away illness or disease. There is no potion that when mixed in a cauldron, put in a vial, and sold by a healer is a panacea to pain. When we distort the truth of healing and try to change the word "healing" into "cure," we get lost and disoriented, and may do more harm than good to each other.

Cary Rayson is a licensed clinical social worker. I met her a year after we launched Magdalene. She asked me some hard and good questions about the program and agreed to come on board as a grant writer and an advocate for the women. She was adamant that we never promise any of the women coming into the community more than could be delivered. Cary knew that such promises would reinforce the disappointments that many of the women had experienced when they were children.

For about a year the community offered outreach to the women walking the streets of Nashville. We made casseroles and offered small tote bags full of essentials like toothbrushes and tampons to women trying to survive under bridges and in alleys. Several of the women who received the gifts dropped everything to enter the community and get clean. As the community became established, our waiting list started growing. Cary recommended that we stop street outreaches because it seemed cruel to tell women on the streets about the Magdalene homes when we couldn't offer them an immediate spot. This lesson translates well into the issue of truth telling in healing. If I promise you the moon and offer you a wafer, even if the wafer is good, it will taste bitter. The bad snake oil salesman will say, "I can give you the moon." The good snake oil salesman would say, "I can give you a wafer, and it might help you imagine the moon."

Discerning good snake oil salesmen also requires examining their desire for power. Healers and power don't go well together. Bad snake oil salesmen and faith healers can be a lethal combination. Faith healers didn't help the reputation of the church at all. Once the snake oil salesmen joined forces with charismatic faith leaders, the yeast was added to the flour of trickery and abuse bubbled over. The healers claimed magical powers and took money for their services. They used snake oil for their own gain, not for the wellness of others, thus tainting the practice with pain and misuse.

Let me be clear: People of faith do heal. They are part of an unbroken line that stretches back to the first time someone saw pain and reached out with a compassionate and loving soul. Many of those healers have used natural medicines to ply their art. Their stories moved into the category folklore as people recounted their experiences to friends and neighbors. They keep the art alive through the ages. Those good people are like old-school faith healers or legitimate snake oil salesmen. They aren't cashing in on healing for fame or power; they simply use their skills and talents to help people.

Separating healers and con artists by the kinds of oils and methods they use is not a bad way to separate the wheat from the chaff or the sheep from the goats. The separation is not meant to condemn or to judge. The point of discernment is to gain wisdom, protect others, and free ourselves. We can be offered a snake oil by a peddler, shake the dust off our heels, and walk away toward a healing balm that lives in the more mysterious places of our lives. We don't have to throw the possibility of healing out with the bad snake oils. There are balms that soothe our souls and bodies, and embracing them is a gift in this world.

Discerning what is good medicine is an integral part of the healing arts. Like learning the art of dating or finding the right spiritual path, the process cannot be laid out in two or three steps. It's more nuanced and variegated. But we can all take steps to help ease the path we navigate.

The first step is to trust your own instincts. If you feel as if someone is coercing you, take a step back and listen to yourself for a minute.

Second, stay close to people you trust. If your family and friends are telling you a path you're considering seems dangerous or isolating, take the time to listen to them. Whenever we face a life-threatening illness, pain, or loss, we can become desperate for healing. While seeking out a new path of healing can be noble, keep the people who love you close on that path. I recently took a walk through the woods with an old friend. He shared his experience of going to see a healer in Brazil and being in the presence of a force of light. He described standing in a current of love where the only tools the healer needed were herbs infused with prayers. The image was both hopeful and scary. As he talked I thought about how if I made such a journey I would want my husband or a trusted friend close by. I would want to have the experience of being bathed in light, but not getting burned by it.

Finally, take as holistic an approach as you can fathom.

This seems so basic, but sometimes when we are in pain our vision and scope narrow. All we can see is the pain. We want to alleviate the pain as quickly as possible, so it's hard to keep in mind that solutions to some chronic issues require more time to take root. Keep in mind that how you eat, drink, bathe, exercise, pray, breathe, talk, walk, and sleep affect every part of you. Ask your doctor how he or she feels about all of those things and have meaningful conversations. I have several friends who suffer from irritable bowel syndrome, and while most have found the greatest healing through working with their doctor, they are, at the same time, working to amend their lives.

One young woman I know went to a homeopathic healer for continued problems with her stomach. She has been on a regular prescription of Western medicine for years. She watched her diet, exercised like a champ, and yet she still suffered a great deal. The healer said that she needed a snake oil and gave her a tincture of oils that would relieve her suffering. The tincture contained actual oil from snakes, and the healer said that people with digestive problems are dealing with snake issues. My friend loved the experience and felt cared for by the tincture she received. She was willing to have acupuncture, tinctures, prayers, and medicine to be able to eat without pain. That is faith and healing working together for her wholeness of body, mind, and spirit.

We have what we need to take on the journey toward healing. We have the loving presence of our creator. We have a healing faith that will not abandon us in our pain or in our fear. The gifts of creation found in oils, teas, and tinctures are good companions to carry along the way. Good friends and kind, healing people are invaluable. I am still learning how to walk this way. As I get older and my body keeps changing, I sometimes worry that something might be wrong with me. It's humbling to notice the changes, and I have talked with older women friends to hear their stories.

Through talking with my friends and my kind doctor and listening to my own voice, I keep striving to maintain a healthy perspective. I continue to learn what a body that's produced three children should experience. The healers I want walking with me are compassionate about the changes. And what seems strange or embarrassing is really kind of funny when it's shared. I want them to see me in a holistic way that incorporates good medicine. Those are the good snake oil salesmen. They know the price they have paid to be healers and the sacrifice they have made in their offerings to fellow pilgrims.

Chapter Seven

LADIES IN CAT SUITS

Luxury Blend Oil

2 ounces coconut oil
8 drops tuberose essential oil
6 drops grapefruit essential oil
4 drops golden champa essential oil
2 drops jasmine essential oil

Pour all of these rich and fragrant ingredients into a glass container and whisk for just a few seconds to combine. Transfer them to a glass cruet to use when you need to feel worthy and uplifted. Champa and jasmine are both expensive oils that are hard to find. You can substitute other floral essential oils for these if you need to. Rub the oil on areas of aching muscles and on worn feet and hands.

SNAKE OIL

THERE IS ONE PICTURE of my whole family taken by a professional photographer a few months before my father's accident. My mom got us all dressed up and took us down to a mall and we sat for the photograph as a close family in our Sunday best. It is a beautiful picture of the "before" time. We are all young and smiling. In the picture there is a strange reflection on my father's forehead, a perfect chalice of light. Had he not died, it might have gone unnoticed. My mom used to tell us that he was a light and that the chalice on his head was a sign. I am not sure what it was a sign of, but to me it meant that he was a great healer and priest.

Just as being healed comes at a cost, being a healer can also be costly. Answering the call to become a healer means you are willing to experience empathetic pain and feel others' brokenness. Being a healer means you are willing to walk in the valley of the shadow of death and wonder what it all means. The people I have known who have a powerful healing voice in this world have given up quite a bit to practice their ministry. There is a powerful story in the scripture about how Isaiah is called to serve. Isaiah is given a message to help heal the world—a gift that seems like an incredible privilege, one that many religious leaders would crave. But when God gives Isaiah the words, Isaiah says, "Woe is me." He stands back, and finally, as a lament, utters, "Here I am, Lord, send me."[1]

The weight of being called by God to serve is a privilege, but don't underestimate the hardship of that service. The privilege of helping to heal a hurting world can be overwhelming at times. Answering the call to heal means our lives will change and lead us to places we have never been before. Healers are on a path of intimacy with God that is murky. I remember when I first stood in a field by the side of the road and thought that I had finally stumbled into a place where I was ready to take on my role as a healing presence in the world. I was searching for thistles to make products when I happened upon a huge field of them. I pulled my car over to the side of the road and marveled at the huge harvest in front of me. After I got some old grocery sacks out of the back of the car and headed into the field, I noticed the few cars going by slowing down to make sure that I was okay. They saw me standing in the middle of a field of half-dead thistles, and I guess they worried either for my safety or for my sanity. To them I was a middle-aged woman staring at a bunch of weeds. To me, I was imbibing the wonder of a rich field of promise. That's when I realized that I had truly become a thistle farmer, a precursor to evolving into a healing snake oil salesman.

Being a thistle farmer is a way of walking into the troubled fields of the world. As a thistle farmer, I find that the world becomes a plentiful field with no borders, owners, or strangers, a place where everything can be used for healing. Anyone can harvest thistles, and when you can see the beauty and value of the thistle, it is easy to remember that there is nothing in all of creation left to be condemned.

I had found the tools in my own medicine box. I had the stories of Moses, Isaiah, Russ, my mom, the women of Magdalene, and many great teachers. Magdalene had been up and running and serving the community for eleven years, and I finally, clearly, saw that the gifts of healing are not just relegated to faith leaders and snake oil salesmen, but that they are for all of us.

The revelation that we are all healers, all heirs of Isaiah's "Here I am," doesn't make the fear or reservations go away. By the beginning of 2010, Thistle Farms was growing into full stature as a voice for women's freedom, so we needed a place big enough to produce millions of dollars' worth of all-natural healing products a year. We found a building and raised well over a million dollars to buy the property. After we purchased the real estate, which includes four storefronts, a manufacturing facility, and offices, we realized the huge responsibility that we had just signed on for. The property needed so much work, and growing the company demanded more effort on our part. We realized we had just taken the first step in a really long journey that appeared to be heading uphill. There is a sacred irony in being thistle farmers and having the deed to a million-dollar building. It is a testimony to the dreams of a community, but when the news sunk in, we all felt like Isaiah, unworthy of this new calling.

If we use the tools we have been given with good intention, declare, "Here I am," and step into the long line of healers in a hurting world, then what? It's a lot for us to take on the role of believing we can be a part of healing the whole world, even one person at a time. Longing and dreaming of changing the world are daunting in the light of our waking truth. Healing pulls us in deeper, and while that is great news it means we have given up some control of our lives. It isn't a sweet reflection that fits neatly into our lives. It's not about getting something you've wanted for a long time, or a dream come true. It's not about success or failure. Being healers means our lives will never be the same. It takes the rest of our lives to practice our craft and then share it with our children and our students so that it can live beyond us. Being a true healer in this world, I believe, costs us our whole lives. I want to be in the line of healers who, without much fuss, offer their prayers and gifts to help ease the pain of others. I hope all of us reach into our medicine boxes and walk into wide-open fields and find the healing that is available to us.

One of the responsibilities of good healers is to teach their truth to others so they, in turn, can pass that knowledge to the next generation. I met a great healer named Joe Howard the year before I entered seminary. I moved into his basement with two other interns who had come to Washington, DC, to live and work in community with a vow of poverty. Joe was an outdoor educator in the state of Maryland, right outside of DC, in the days before outdoor educators were cool. His mantra was "If you want to preserve the wilderness, teach a child to love it."

Joe taught children to love the woods that he loved so much. When I started working, I knew there was something special and kind of mystical about him, in the most practical sense of the word. He was the embodiment of unaffected compassion for the earth as well as her occupants. He spent time every day teaching us about his beloved wilderness. He would make us name trees before we could eat dinner. He explained to us the importance of having a stick pile separate from the compost, and he gave lectures on the evils of plastic. Over and over, he taught us why he loved the wilderness. He wanted us to learn how to love the woods well.

To this day, when I walk in the hills of Tennessee filled with sweet sassafras and tulip poplars, love overflows in me. I have so much gratitude for Joe Howard and his willingness to teach me all the details of the wilderness. His healing love for the earth has nearly cost him his life. The acts he performed to heal and preserve the planet included developing a park around the biggest live oak tree in Maryland, holding contests for the largest trees in every county, and picking up trash along the road near Rock Creek Parkway. Several years ago, he was bent over the side of the road gathering trash when a car struck him. His broken body survived, and after many surgeries and the gift of leg braces, beautiful Joe Howard returned to the roadside, picking up trash and teaching people to love the woods.

It is the same if we want to preserve faith: we need to teach our children to love it. We teach our children the faith that was passed down to us, we teach them what justice and truth mean to us, and we help form the faith that will grow in them. Part of what I claim as my faith is a gift from people who loved me enough to teach me about their path. That's what we do. We hear the stories, we try to live into them, and we spend our lives teaching children as best we can what it means to carry the faith on. We learn that wherever we go, we show with our actions what healing looks like. We give drink to the thirsty and food to the hungry, clothe the naked, visit the imprisoned, comfort the sorrowful, tend the sick, and bury the dead. We mix clove with olive oil and put it on our babies, we pick up trash, and we rub tobacco on a sting, all to show we have healing. Generation after generation learns that this passing is a great gift. It takes us a lifetime to learn and more than a lifetime to share our knowledge with the next generation.

Each of my teachers led me on a journey that not only carried me forward but also led me back thousands of years to the roots of oils. The history of oils is as deep and legendary as the history of faith and politics. It's full of lore, old wives' tales, and the most mystical and wondrous stories the holy writ has to offer.

I remember when I first noticed the mayapples blooming on the forest floors in Tennessee. I was talking to my friend Tara about them—she knows the woods like the back of her hand—and she explained that they are used for healing warts. "How did they figure that out?" I asked.

"Their moms told them, I bet," my friend replied. I was silent for a bit, trying to figure out in my mind where along the motherline we had lost the knowledge that mayapples cured warts.

I learned so much from those who have gone before me as well as from researching, experimenting, and watching others choose oils to blend to enhance their scent and healing properties. Becoming a seller of oils is not a journey you make quickly or lightly or alone. I have had guides who were willing to spend whole afternoons with me, talking about one kind of plant. The instinct to want to learn more and help others was surely planted in me when I sat with Mr. Price on the stone wall in the side yard on those long afternoons contemplating what it all means. The events, people, and places are separate threads that weave together with a thousand other threads to make a tapestry whose theme is healing and whose images are of old snake oil jars that instruct us to pour them over our bodies to help soothe mind and spirit.

Those who want to answer the call to become good healers probably also need to pray. Prayer is central to healing. Healers learn how to pray and then teach others the words and thoughts they cherish. We learn to pray at the feet of teachers who show us how to pray by example. The prayer attributed to St. Francis is central to my life of prayer. It reads:

> LORD, *make us instruments of your peace. Where there is hatred, let us sow love; where there is injury, pardon; where there is discord, union; where there is doubt, faith; where there is despair, hope; where there is darkness, light; where there is sadness, joy. Grant that we may not so much seek to be consoled as to console; to be understood as to understand; to be loved as to love. For it is in giving that we receive; it is in pardoning*

that we are pardoned; and it is in dying that we are born to eternal life. Amen.²

The prayer isn't boastful or proud, but it calls us back to the center. I have placed the prayer at the end of every Sunday service over which I have presided for the past twenty years. After hearing the words week after week, I believe the petition is written on my children's hearts.

Those who desire to heal carry prayer as one of the most important tools in their medicine box. The Lord's Prayer is the most common prayer in the Christian faith, and one Jesus offers the disciples when they ask him to teach them to pray. This prayer becomes part of the people who pray it every day. I have sat at many beds and whispered this prayer with dying disciples and their beloved gathered around them. I remember praying this prayer when my mom died. She had lost almost all of her language, but if I started the Lord's Prayer, she would pray alongside me, even when she had forgotten that the priest was her daughter. The prayer had become part of her. Years before, she taught the prayer to us, and we offered it back. The prayers we offer our whole lives become part of us, and we share them with our children, and then they offer them back to us when we can't say them ourselves. My husband and I have taught the Lord's Prayer to our children, and I know someday my boys will say that prayer and the prayer of St. Francis over me when I need it.

Healing continues generation after generation as each

generation learns how to do loving acts. If we want to save the woods, we teach our children to love them. If we want to keep our family, we teach our children to love it. If we want to continue in the faith, we teach our children to pray. We have been given a beautiful gift of faith, commissioned and anointed by the generation before, to love the world as our own. We keep the art of healing alive by anointing healers ready to take on this facet of love for the world.

Church theology teaches that we don't always believe what we pray. Instead, we pray what we hope to believe. We keep doing the right thing, showing gratitude through our actions, surrendering to our faith, and trusting the rest will come our way. No one can walk for us; we have to do it ourselves. We won't be religious healers if we never do the work. We are born with everything we need for the healing journey, but the gifts we receive at birth need to be cultivated, honed, and trained. We must write moral laws on our hearts and memorize sacred texts that can become mantras. We need to practice the tenets of faith to the best of our ability so that, when called upon, we can reach into our medicine chests with some grace and assurance for the sake of love.

Those who want to be good healers also would do well to recognize the challenges of the work. The world we live in is filled with busyness, and people don't necessarily want to hear more words. A great theologian and lover of the poor in England, F. D. Maurice, wrote that the business of commerce makes it hard to have an interior life and reflect on the gifts offered to us by the church. More than 150 years later, we live in a world with more global connections and ways to fill our day with information than ever before. We also live in a world that has been at war for years. None of my children has a conscious memory of a world without war. This is also a world that has been sickened by the abuse of people in power—people who have used faith to hurt others and who are stifled by their own grieving and pain. Speaking peace into this harsh world is hard. It makes it harder when you have to speak about not what you believe, but what you hope to believe. The words you use are spoken knowing that if we pray the words over and over, it will help form what we believe.

Those who strive to be good healers must also come to terms with what they have to work with. Healers, especially those in not-for-profits and church work, have to get used to tools like thistles, dirt, spit, and broken pieces. Embracing those things and having the eyes to see them as valuable give the work dignity. At Thistle Farms we have become familiar with makeshift shelving, used office furniture, and discarded coffee mugs. When we moved into the building we had no budget for furniture and equipment, and were ready to work off the floor if we needed to. Holli Anglin, the managing director of Thistle Farms, has what we call beatific eyes. She can take mismatched furniture and an old coffeepot and make the most beautiful office space. She sees beauty where others see discarded items.

Another trait that helps with being a good healer is the ability to work in community. That allows all people with visions and dreams to bring ideas to the table and create something magical that no one person could have imagined alone. I never could have imagined what Thistle Farms has become. It has taken the organizational skills of people like Carole Hagan, Carolyn Snell, and Anna Stratstrom, who came as volunteers and had ideas and visions for entire departments like the papermaking studio, the sewing cooperative, the social media division, and the home parties. Each person brought to the community a distinct pair of eyes and a fresh story to enhance all our lives.

If you hold on to an idea just because it is yours, the vision will not grow and your ability to serve the world will suffer. Many years ago we used to name all the products after biblical characters: the salt scrub was called Lot's Wife, the lotion was called Hannah's Laughter, and so on and so forth. A marketing team advised us to get rid of all the names and simplify our message. It was hard to let the product names go; I had spent hours with a couple of others thinking about them, but I knew the marketing team was right. We need to work together to be better healers.

The old snake oils developed a bad name not necessarily because the oils were bad but because of the claims made by their sellers. The oils themselves have been around forever, and they will continue to offer their gifts if we can learn their lessons.

The healing arts change every time a new spice is discovered or when someone stumbles on a new herb in an old-growth forest. Healing oils changed dramatically after the invention of the steam-distillation process, which releases plant properties in distilled liquid form. The techniques and ingredients change as we grow and learn and heal and then reach out to try to ease the suffering of a friend. I still feel like a novice in making and selling oils for healing, in part because it's a lifelong quest.

Good healers are patient. They are willing to take their time to learn how to use oils for specific purposes. Healers have to remember that mint and lavender hold different properties. Each has its appropriate place and time for use. When we rush, we slip up by making the oils too strong or choosing an oil that is counterproductive to the ailment we are trying to help soothe. Good healers are humble. They know that they will ply their art with various outcomes. Such humility doesn't make them less courageous in their willingness to try to soothe people; it just makes them not boastful or proud. Being humble means not taking anything for granted and being willing to learn about healing every time you offer oils and prayers. Good healers know how to listen, how to forgive themselves and others, and how to learn from older and better healers who are willing to share their knowledge.

Good healers would do well to learn about commissioning, the idea that each of us is set aside, or appointed, for a particular task. Commissioning is a time when you pull out oils like frankincense and myrrh and anoint the one being commissioned. The idea that we are charged with the responsibility to go out to heal the world is an old truth. Most of us are appointed over and over in our lives as we learn more about what the gift of healing looks like for us. We are sent out repeatedly with God's blessing to love. It is a holy journey, and in all faiths we have to make the pilgrimage with practically nothing. Go out and serve the world, and take nothing—walking stick, purse, or sandals. In every commissioning, that is a similar theme. We come into this world with nothing, and we leave with nothing. There's an old saying, "You never see a U-haul behind a hearse." That is how we healers live, how we love, and how we journey toward God. We are anointed to go out again and again to try to love the world until we get it right. It's helpful, though, to get some good direction in where to seek out true teachers and good medicine. This always takes time and intention.

Forging a new path on our own is nearly impossible. We learn from a variety of faith traditions. From the eightfold path given to the Buddha in the shade of the Bodhi tree, we learn how peace is a part of healing. Commandments handed down to Moses on Mount Sinai guide us. Teachings given to Mohammed by Allah in the desert explain how we should make pilgrimages to seek healing and wisdom. Teachings in Hinduism have influenced the way we treat animals and reach for deeper meaning. These traditions are so basic that it seems redundant to repeat them, but it is surprising how many intelligent people discard entire faiths without even cracking the spine of a text to see what they're about. Moving beyond our boundaries to realize a universal God is inevitable when we practice our faith regularly. It is good to begin our walk in healing by doing and by reading and reflecting on the best sources, knowing that the more we learn, the better healers we will become.

We are called to learn to be healers; we learn everything we can and commission the next generation to continue the art and practice of healing, and the rest we leave up to love. That is more than enough to make our lives full and rich. There isn't a better example of this abundance in healing than the height of the blackberry season in Nashville, Tennessee. There are plenty of blackberries to harvest, but the laborers are few. Chiggers love blackberry fields, and the blackberries have plenty of briars. They tend to grow in wild and unruly places and fruit in the hottest days of the summer season. For $3.99, you can go down to the local grocery store and buy a quart of blackberries. It is tempting to forgo the picking. In the same way, we forgo going into the world and nature to discover healing. It's too hard. Let's just go to a pharmacy instead and take a pill. We decide that we just don't want to go out there again and pick blackberries. We think it's too costly and not a good use of our time.

But to not go is to miss the joy of the blackberry. If you don't go, you will miss those clear summer afternoons in the hills of Tennessee, when a hawk soars right overhead and shadows you like a benediction. You will miss the smell of the air. You will miss that flutter in your heart when something rustles nearby and you have no idea if it is a chipmunk or a snake. You will miss the embodiment of the truth that grace is free. When you pick a blackberry straight from the bush and eat it, you can feel the healing. You don't come back from picking blackberries without rejoicing that you feel better. The journey itself is the gift. It is a loving gift from a God who has compassion and love for us, who knows that when we go out with each other—to Africa, Ecuador, the hills of Tennessee, wherever we are—all we need for healing is nearby.

Finally, being a good healer requires action. Without action, the idea of healing is just an ideal as lofty as heaven and as thin as a cloud. All dreams fade with the morning light, and all intention without action becomes a memory. To be a good healer you have to implement the ideals of healing. If I had just had a sweet vision of a sanctuary but hadn't lifted a finger, the inspiration, like all muses, would have passed me by. I am so grateful for the image of the lady in the cat suit. She called me to action. That image keeps me going as a snake oil salesman sometimes. She reminds me to be as dogged about striving for justice and healing as others are about power and wealth. She reminds me to never give up and to continue to pursue what I believe. That is faith to me—to keep hoping and asking and trying and trusting that love will have the last word always. That is why I will keep stirring the pots of oils with lavender and a slurry of thistle. Sometimes the oils just take a good while to sink all the way into our heart.

Chapter Eight

INCANTATIONS

A *Winter Balm*
(With a Heartfelt Incantation)

8 teaspoons 100 percent shea butter
8 teaspoons aloe vera oil
4 teaspoons beeswax
8 drops cinnamon leaf essential oil
4 drops clove essential oil

Melt the shea butter in a pan over low heat.
Add the aloe vera oil, then combine with the
beeswax and cinnamon leaf and clove oils.
This thick, rich balm is perfect for winter
because there is nothing more healing for the
skin than cinnamon and clove. This balm
protects and boosts our system. Before you
apply the balm, pull out your favorite book
of poetry and read a poem. Choose one line

from the poem that speaks to your heart.
Repeat the line several times and let it sink
into you like the balm itself.

I HAVE ALWAYS ENJOYED going barefoot. I love everything
about feeling the ground directly under my feet. When I
was a child I took pride in being able to walk all the way to
the corner market in the middle of summer with no shoes. I
danced over the clover-filled yard with plenty of honeybees
hidden among the blossoms and traversed blacktops so hot
they looked like rippling water on the horizon. Everyone in
my family went barefoot, and my mom had the toughest
feet of all. Her heels were so calloused that she snagged
panty hose with them. She could walk barefoot into the
snow to take out the trash without feeling the cold. I was
told I had tough feet, and to keep my feet tough I had to
keep going barefoot. If I went a whole winter with shoes,
by spring my feet would be tender. Going barefoot was a
fun habit that kept my soles tough.

When I was ordained, I was eight and a half months
pregnant, and the only shoes I could wear were clogs.
Whenever possible, I would kick off the clogs and walk
barefoot. I haven't found a good reason to put my shoes
back on. My only concern with preaching barefoot is not
offending or distracting people because my feet are sticking
out. Many cathedrals and chapels across the country hang
images of Jesus over or behind the altar, either on the cross
or resurrected, and in those images, he's barefoot. Taking

off shoes as we step into a sanctuary is a ritual that readies us to walk on holy ground.

Many religious sanctuaries ask their adherents to remove their shoes before entering. There are even pieces of religious furniture sold explicitly to hold shoes. Walking into a Hindu temple and seeing the beaded mules left by well-dressed worshipers is a religious experience in and of itself. Seeing all the Tevas and Birkenstocks piled by the front door at a meditation chapel in the Tennessee hills speaks volumes about the earthly pilgrims visiting. At the alabaster mosque in Egypt thousands of shoes are left in long, neat rows out front. They are signs of the endless parade of pilgrims and tourists who for a thousand years have been willing to abandon them in search of the sacred.

Kicking off your shoes to pray is an ancient practice. The act connects us down to the earth, keeps the sanctuary clean, and harkens back to Moses walking barefoot toward the fiery bush. The ritual readies us for prayer. It wakes us up to get us out of our ruts and invites us to step quietly into this space of prayer. In a prayerful and humble position, we're ready to receive and give love.

A few years ago, I preached barefoot for a flower festival at a cathedral in St. Louis. Thousands of blossoms filled the space with fragrance and beauty. Fragrant roses, gardenias, and lilies blended together, transforming the sanctuary into a sweet bouquet. The service was dedicated to the beauty of the earth and the gift of flowers. I stood in a tall, creaky, hundred-year-old wooden pulpit preaching about the lilies, thistles, roses, and irises of creation. When I finished, I realized I had spoken the entire sermon standing on my toes. My calves felt like they might spasm as I descended the steps. I was poised on the fulcrum between laughter and tears and opted for a silent *Thank you.* I was grateful God granted me the gift of feeling the beauty of creation—all the way down to my toes!

Developing rituals such as not wearing shoes, crossing yourself, kneeling, and placing your palms together are reminders to take a healing posture. Rituals place us in a healing position. They alert us that we are setting aside a specific time and place for something special. Along with most of these physical rituals, words accompany the posture. The words are familiar phrases, like incantations, that conjure up the sacredness of the moment. Incantations are like calls to prayer, responses, and words repeated in liturgy. These sayings help center and move us into sacred space. I use the term "incantation" like I use the term "snake oil." I take both of those old terms and peel back layers of culture and meaning to rediscover and reconnect with very simple and earthly ideas of faith and healing.

Prayers, mantras, and rhythms allow us to speak to where we are and what our intentions should be. A muezzin recites the *adhān* from minarets five times a day around the world to tell everyone to stop, turn, and begin the ritual of prayer. Driving around Cairo, you hear a multitude of voices slightly out of sync echo the call to prayer. One of the most basic incantations in the mainline Christian church is "The Lord be with you." The response, "And also with you," can silence an entire crowd. The words mean "Be quiet, this is the time to pray." But those words also hint that the buffet is ready, too. These ancient words call us to a more peaceful place.

Many incantations were introduced to us in childhood and have been repeated to us many times. As soon as the phrase is uttered, we know what is happening and what is coming. Far less religious incantations for children include "Olly, olly, oxen free," "Abracadabra," "Once upon a time," and "Long ago, far away." None of my kids learned those incantations exactly. My oldest used to start every story with "Long away and far ago." My middle son used to say, "Once a bitty time," and my youngest, when I would say, "Once upon a time," would yell, "But I don't want to go to bed!" The sentence incited begging to stay up a little bit longer.

Even as adults, we know that when a friend says, "You better not tell," what follows won't be good. "I hate to bother you," means a heavier workload will follow the conversation. "You gotta hear this," means my husband or son has written a new melody, and I need to drop what I'm doing and listen.

Our incantation in the daily Thistle Farms circle developed without any discussion or council. Over the course of years, as we welcomed new women every day, from every station of life, we starting saying, "Welcome to the circle," in unison after someone introduced herself. A group visiting recently from Atlanta said that one of the most powerful things they carried away from the day of immersion into the community was the "welcome to the circle" phrase. They said that every member of their group felt included and welcomed. They wished their church could extend this kind of hospitality. "Welcome to the circle" says so much in such a simple phrase. It's the perfect incantation for our community. No one quite remembers when we all started saying it in unison.

Incantations are woven into the fabric of civil rights movements. Using common chants and call-and-response helps unite a crowd. When I lived in Washington, DC, I regularly went to protests. I loved going with my friends to the Pentagon, the Capitol, and the South African Embassy. Each protest featured signs and symbols, and the best protests used powerful chants that were repeated louder and louder in perfect rhythm with passion as we walked in circles. Those incantations rang in our ears hours after we had left for dinner.

Once, we were called to go to the National Geographic headquarters because a dignitary was visiting and we wanted to protest his attendance. We arrived and started chanting with other marchers: "Jonas, Jonas, you can't hide. We know you're on apartheid's side." Over and over we yelled this incantation. Some people in long khaki overcoats with earphones in their ears started taking pictures. I became nervous when I realized I had no idea who Jonas was or who was taking my picture. I leaned over to a nearby protestor and asked, "Who is Jonas?" I had gotten caught up in the chant itself, enlisted by its power and moved by its rhythms. The chanting was such a powerful and moving ritual that I didn't even have to know the meaning of it to be swept up by it.

Incantations stir up stuff in our hearts and minds as the phrases are repeated. As soon as someone says, "Though I walk through the valley of death," our emotions begin to stir. Whenever my mind wanders to that famous line from Psalm 23, I can't help but think of the many funerals I have sat through and presided over. I picture the green hills of Tennessee and how sweet it is to walk through those hills and valleys with a loving God. That is why our liturgy is full of incantations that let us know what is happening around us and recall old and powerful sayings that have been repeated since our ancestors were given the Torah. The incantations used in healing are part of the larger tradition of ritualized phrases used to conjure up a sense of sacred space in the middle of our ordinary days. The incantations, chants, and prayers are like old music that readies us for worship. When we hear the first few notes of a favorite old song, we're taken back to a certain time and place and can feel our hearts starting to sing along. Incantations include familiar phrases in music, old rhythms, and repeated movements that get us into a sacred frame of mind, as well as old phrases healers have been using in the backcountry for years as part of their healing rituals.

I first stumbled on some of these old incantations from my sister's *Foxfire* books, a series about the old ways of Appalachia, which included a whole section on faith healers. Along with stories of how people were miraculously cured, snapshots appeared on each page showing faces of people who looked like sundried fruit. Each person interviewed claimed some pretty specific healing abilities, and each had his or her own phrases and rituals to help the healing process. Every page described someone near death from a snakebite or falling into a fire and how these healers used their skills to save that person. Almost all the healers in the book used scripture as they laid hands on a suffering friend who was about to die from thrush, bleeding, or a burn.

Several used the phrase from Ezekiel 16 in which God says to his servant, "Live! And grow up like a plant of the field," as their own incantation for healing to commence.[1] Many of them used their breath to "call out the fire" or "pull out the thrush." To call out the fire means to help soothe a burn. The homemade remedies from local healers were mixed with touch and spoken word and then offered for free to their community. Those stories always reminded me of Joe Howard and how he had to repeat himself all the time to help us understand.

Knowing a few incantations and calls to prayer helps me as a chaplain find a way to be fully present with people. I once visited a young man in a hospital who was not very religious, and I felt like I was imposing. His parents, whom I've pastored for years, asked me to come. I didn't want to intrude, but I also wanted to be faithful to my duties as a priest. I brought him oil, and he let me touch his feet and pray. The next time I visited, I brought my small communion kit—which includes miniature shot glasses for wine, a wafer, as well as a small stole and paten. I asked if I could serve him communion. He accepted. I began with a very short prayer and then recited the words from the Eucharistic prayer: "On the night before he was handed over to suffering and death, our Lord Jesus Christ gathered his disciples around the table..." On cue about six young men who were friends of his walked into the room. When they saw us standing around the hospital bed in prayer, they knew exactly what was happening because they recognized the familiar words. They joined us, and we broke bread in communion with words two thousand years old—sung, read, and passed down.

Walking away from the hospital, I started thinking about all the things we do and all the incantations we use to try to feel protected. Certain invocations are etched into our memory to help us feel connected to God and at peace with our circumstances. Every person has different ones and we all have them. We knock on wood and utter sayings like "Cross your fingers" and "My lucky stars" and the serenity prayer. At its root, "God willin' and the creek don't rise!" is not all that different from "Inshallah." Both are said to remind us that we and those we love are in safe and loving hands. My mom used to believe that we needed to say our prayers at night before bed in order for us to be safe. She also believed that we needed to kneel down beside the bed for the prayers to be done properly and with enough humility. It wasn't enough to say them in bed. She drilled these incantations into me so much that even on the very few occasions I stumbled into my college dorm room a bit dizzy after midnight, I always slid down to my knees before crawling up into the bed. I needed to say the prayers, as much out of love and respect for my mom as out of the desire to say the prayers themselves. Those prayers were the incantations I carried from my childhood that brought me safely into adulthood. The idea of incantations is simply old and familiar prayers and sayings that help us to be open to healing in faith.

My husband's uncle Norm lived in New Mexico. A few years ago my husband and I drove our boys out west so that they could visit Norm, who was pretty sick. He had spent years directing the Peace Corps throughout Africa and had many stories to tell. He had a treasure box full of rocks and old coins he had collected on his journey, and when we visited he would take the treasures out one by one and share a rich story about his adventures. He would then talk about all the places that he and his wife, Fran, and his daughter, Crystal, had visited in New Mexico, including some of the old mission churches and historical spots. On one visit, we to made a day trip to visit Chimayó, an old mission that was the site of a miracle.

In the early 1800s, a friar there was praying when he saw a light bursting from a hillside. He followed the light and, digging on the hillside, found a crucifix that he believed to be miraculous. He and his flock brought this miraculous crucifix to the nearest church, several miles away in Santa Cruz, but three times it disappeared and was discovered back in its hole on the hillside. After the third episode, they built a small chapel on the site. Then the miraculous healings began. El Santuario de Chimayó is now known as the "Lourdes of America." The crucifix still resides on the chapel altar, and a sacred sand pit sits nearby, behind the main altar. More than three hundred thousand people visit this small dirt hole annually.

The prayer room, which is located in the sacristy of the church, is lined with hundreds of discarded crutches and braces and handmade shrines. When my family traveled there, I noticed my two younger sons in the line to scoop a little of the dirt into a plastic holder. They wanted to take a bit of the sacred ground with them. I loved that my sons believed in the miraculous nature of this bit of dirt, and I put five dollars in the donation box. One of the boys still has the box of dirt on his desk, and I am sure it brings him comfort and memories and sends his mind to a sweet space. The dirt is like an incantation that grounds him and sets him in a special time and place.

Sacred sites and holy places allow us to feel the divine presence all around the world. People have been traveling to the waters of Lourdes, the Wailing Wall, and Mecca for centuries to hear the old prayers, touch the sacred, and journey among the faithful. We can imagine the old prayers, oils, dirt, and water being passed around, sold, and used,

all for the hope of healing. Incantations are often part of
the rituals at sacred sites. It is a meaningful journey to visit
those places and breathe in the spirit around them.

The Fisk Memorial Chapel at Fisk University is a holy
site for me. Every once in a while I visit Fisk's campus,
pass under the archway that declares ESTABLISHED 1866 TO
EDUCATE FREED SLAVES, and settle into a corner of the chapel. When I sit close to the rafters I feel like I can hear in
a sacred whisper the old rhythms and words spoken and
repeated by many generations. The air feels thick with a
mixture of lemon wax and moss. The octagonal walls carry
a residue of hope and despair in lingering prayers. Even in
the pews, constructed shortly after the Civil War, I can feel
the handiwork of the spirit and hear the echoes of old songs
coming from the wood grain and the quiet ceiling fans.

The same sacred songs have been sung by the faithful
worshipers in the Fisk Memorial Chapel for more than 150
years. Hymns like "Amazing Grace" and "Lift Every Voice
and Sing" have echoed in this space thousands of times over,
powerful incantations calling worshipers to believe again.
You can imagine the singing and the speeches during the
civil rights movement filling the students with the power to
want to lay down their lives for the cause. You can sense
your own need to hear the words to the songs once more in
order to leave revived and ready to do the next right thing.

Sometimes when I go, I am so scared I will run into
someone who will ask, *What are you doing in here listening to
this beautiful air?* I know it will never happen, but I also
respect the fear itself. Such healthy, holy fear reminds me

I have no right to the gifts of the Spirit, and that I should always tread softly and slowly where the Spirit is thick.

When we use homeopathic snake oils with ritualized words, the oils take on more soothing spiritual qualities. Incantations become a prelude to the anointing; they set the stage and the heart for what is coming next. Without incantations, rituals and anointing with oil would seem too abrupt and intrusive. The art of healing has a natural rhythm. The encounter usually begins with a conversation in which you learn the nature of the problem, the desire of the other person, and the level of openness and comfort the person has for what is coming next. This is a big part of the healing process. If you ignore the person's needs and fears, the ritual is pointless. If you are completely engrossed in your own actions you tend to get tripped up, and the experience feels forced or awkward. This process allows you to get your own nerves and ego out of the way. The beginning conversation tends to calm the room and settles the spirits of the giver and the receiver.

When you feel peace settling over a room, it's probably a good time to recite an incantation or two. This can be reciting a Psalm like 42 or 139 or taking a moment to read a passage from a sacred text. I believe reading from sacred texts is the most peaceful way to start a healing ritual. My incantation is a blend of prayers in the Book of Common Prayer with offerings of thanksgiving and petition.

In beginning of the healing rite I always try to offer

something specific about the healing hoped for by the receiver and to pray for mercy and forgiveness. I begin by laying my hands on the person and saying, "I lay my hands on you, beseeching our Lord to sustain you with the Holy Spirit, so that you never forget the healing power of love." As the words are spoken, peace washes over the room. The act of laying your hands on someone who is sick or vulnerable is powerful. As if on cue, a new silence rises as cluttered thoughts are cleared and old fears are set aside. The act of touching and reciting an incantation can bring up tears from deep reservoirs. The scene reminds us that life is full of mystery and that we are not bound by only hard facts. The words offered in my opening prayers are an expression of deep hope, which I offer in love. I am grateful for the words.

As I recite the words I usually pour a little oil into my hands and then gently press my hands on the other person's forehead, hand, or foot. The oil on my hands against the person's skin gets warmer as we pray. Sometimes people start saying thank you even before the prayer is done. Maybe just the intention of the prayer feels like enough to some people.

One of the kindest women I met during her residency at Magdalene was Pat. She was an athletic and compassionate woman. She couldn't pass a stray animal on the road without wanting to help or refuse anyone in need. She became severely ill with a disease that destroys the liver. She called me from the hospital during a very critical flare-up and asked me to come and say prayers and lay hands on her. "Don't forget your oils," she reminded me. I gathered my prayer book and oils and headed over to see her. She was in the county hospital, which offers little privacy, in what they call a triple—three beds to one room, separated only by thin curtains. I felt self-conscious about praying out loud, so I began to whisper the words. I asked for blessing, comfort, and peace. I prayed that we never forget the healing power of love in our lives and I gave thanks for Pat's gentle spirit and life. Then I got ready to put oil onto her head. In the moment of prayer, Pat lifted her gown and said, "Pour that on my liver, help me, Lord. Heal my liver." Startled to see her naked body, I paused for a second before pouring the oil on the skin over her liver. I loved her for being so direct and calling on God to heal her.

I was once called to a man's bedside in San Eduardo, Ecuador, during one of St. Augustine's annual pilgrimages to the school we founded in my mom's honor in 1998. A man from a rural village had been hit by a car two weeks before, and doctors from a hospital about thirty miles away had removed his leg and then sent him home. The night before I arrived, he had fallen out of bed and reinjured himself. He told us that during the night he had a nightmare about his child crossing the same strip of road, and in his dream he was trying to run to save the child. He was a beautiful young father who made a living as a farmworker. The loss of his leg meant he couldn't provide for his wife and children.

Roberto Cocco, a translator, and I headed over to his house just as the sun was setting. The family had no electricity, and darkness had settled in by the time I approached his bedside. The wife and daughter made vigil on the edge of the bed as Roberto and I kneeled on the ground in front of them. I listened to the man's story as Roberto translated with great compassion and concern. After the conversation, we began to pray as I laid my hand on his forehead with the consecrated oil I had carried with me. Without knowing a word I was saying, his wife started crying and put her hand on his shoulder. Their daughter wrapped herself around him. That broken and fragile prayer at twilight in the Ecuadorian countryside reminds me of the sweetness of incantation that opened a sacred space for us to grieve and pray together.

Whether it's wind singing, water falling, or the honks and groans of animals, nature speaks powerfully in incantations. The owl's call is one of my favorite incantations. I've heard an owl call and spent ten minutes trying to figure out where the sound came from. As soon as the owl sings, the light in the woods changes from dappled to hallowed. The song makes it feel like the ground is sacred, and I need to walk quietly as I search and listen for another call to prayer. The woods are divine, and the owl is part of that creation with his simple incantation to wake up and see the glorious afternoon light.

Setting a tone and a space for healing is part of the job of a good healer, whether in New Mexico, Ecuador, Nashville, or Rwanda. Sometimes it means kicking off your shoes and using the hands that God gave you to help heal some broken situations and hearts. The incantations help set the mood and open the hearts and minds. Healing is the sacred embracing the mundane, the eternal kissing the temporal. Bringing wholeness is unbelievably beautiful, and it requires our whole selves being present in the moment to see and feel it. The best example to me is the way flowers bloom. I can plant the bulbs in the fall, mulch them in the winter, water them in the spring, and still be completely blown away when the first blossoms come. It's not that I forget what a tulip looks like, or that I haven't worked to see it, but when it blossoms, it is so beautiful I can't imagine that its color could be so bright, its petals so soft, or the dramatic black stamen so majestic. The flowering of a plant is a miracle to me.

Incantations offered by prophets and poets live through time and geography and speak deep within us. I know when I hear a faithful incantation that will stir my spirit and wake me up. When Amos cries out, "Let justice roll down like waters and righteousness like an ever-flowing stream,"[2] people will always be moved to act. When Julian of Norwich cries, "All shall be well, and all shall be well and all manner of thing shall be well," we can feel a timeless incantation that can calm our spirits. Every day at Thistle Farms we begin with the simple phrase "Welcome to the circle." My prayer is that the incantation will outlive me. I pray that it will prepare everyone to welcome new strangers into the community for years to come.

Chapter Nine

BACKTRACKING, BACKSLIDING, AND SIDETRACKING

The Best Healing Salve Ever

5 ounces olive oil
¼ cup sliced fresh ginger
1 ounce vitamin E skin oil
20 drops tea tree essential oil
2 tablespoons 100 percent shea butter
2 teaspoons beeswax
15 drops eucalyptus essential oil
10 drops tuberose essential oil

Begin by heating the olive oil in the insert
of a slow cooker. Add the remaining
ingredients and let simmer for 9–10 hours.
Remove the ginger slices, pour into tins, and

let cool. This recipe takes a day to make, but the balm is well worth your time and effort. The mixture helps heal scars, and eases sore muscles, digestion, and breathing.

ALL OF US ARE allowed to start over and to backtrack from time to time to remember who we are and where we come from. This isn't punishment, but a gift. It's like the old game of hopscotch my sister and I spent hours and hours playing on the driveway with a bit of chalk. One afternoon, we drew the board wrong. As we jumped through the first four numbers on the hopscotch board, we realized we had made the squares smaller and smaller as the numbers got higher. It was just about impossible to jump into the last squares with a normal size foot, and honestly, my sister's feet have always been smaller than mine. To make matters worse, we were highly competitive. Any time one of us would even barely touch the smallest edge of the hopscotch square, the other would scream in joy, "You touched the line. Start over!" We kept starting over until my more patient and smaller-footed sister finally made it through.

In my mind it was the best game of hopscotch we ever played. We played and played until finally my sister perfected the game. On the path of healing sometimes we have to start over for the thousandth time, until by some dumb luck and passing grace we hit it just right. That hopscotch game is not a bad metaphor for how we learn to walk in love.

Love's path is never straight and it is never easy. When life circles us back around to a place we've been before, we get to have a closer look. Sometimes circling back for the hundredth time, we finally get close enough to see where we are headed, and it's easier to see the axioms at work. We get to see how love requires surrender, calls us to speak our truth, and asks us to take every step with gratitude. We get to find love in the details. We get to see the elaborate handiwork of love written on the backside of every maple leaf.

I believe that through love, healing is always possible. I believe that healing is possible because love never fails. I also believe that I get so distracted by everything sometimes that I forget I believe those things. When I forget, old fears creep in, and sometimes I have to start over. I have to remember what it is that I believe in the first place. I have to remember love's basic axioms, which form the foundation of all that I believe:

- Love has no beginning or ending.
- Love is the story of God unfolding in our lives.
- Love has no dogma or doctrine, but has a dogged determination to bloom.
- Love is sufficient, even when I am not.

For me, these are the basic rules for love and I use them to ground my faith. They remind me that love is constant, the soul force of the universe, and how we encounter the holy in our daily lives. Taken as a whole, these axioms help make the case that love carries us beyond the narrow path of believing that healing is moving from diagnosis to cure. They move us instead into the wide space of healing. Healing is a natural outcome of love. As we learn how to love, we learn how to heal. Making this case is truly easier said than done, because healing is hard. The axioms of love become difficult to remember when healings come in the middle of the night, when shadows look more real than figures. Love is hard to remember when our prayers feel like puffs of wind that vanish into the thin atmosphere. But when we begin again, we usually remember that love got us through the last time and that love will carry us through the day again. Love is older than Eden; its principles are written into the very fabric of creation.

Nothing makes us question how love heals as much as seeing the injustices of poverty in this world. Poverty rattles the rules of love and troubles our souls. The effects of people suffering without enough food make us wonder if healing as an outcome of love can permeate the hard skin of poverty. The economic troubles of my childhood probably made me more vulnerable to abuse. Poverty is what drives Thistle Farms to partner with other social enterprises that serve people suffering under its burden and the victims of sexual violence. It is so troubling to everything we think we know about healing and values when you see some of the devastating effects that having no resources will wreak on women's lives.

Thistle Farms currently has four working partnerships

in South America, Asia, and Africa. We established our first partnership in Rwanda with a group of women who survived the genocide. It is called Ikerizi. They make healing geranium oils that we buy and mix with our own recipes to sell. The next partnership, in Lwala, Kenya, is with a sewing cooperative attached to the Lwala clinic. This serves a community that has been and continues to be devastated by HIV/AIDS. They sew beautiful bags and clutches. The next partnership came with ABAN, which works with homeless pregnant teenagers in Accra, Ghana. They recycle plastic bags used for drinking water into aprons, bags, and wallets.

With each group we practice a shared-trade model, which goes beyond fair trade and seeks to share the profits we make together. We have plans in place to work with two other groups in different parts of the world that are trying to find ways to alleviate the devastating poverty experienced by women who have been trafficked. We want to design a diaper bag filled with good things for babies and begin to make clothing. The possibilities are endless if women's cooperatives join forces to help expand markets and fight poverty.

Our most challenging partnership so far has been with a women's group in Ecuador. Even after fifteen years of our returning annually to the same small town to run a clinic and help grow a small school, the women's cooperative is only now getting off the ground. It is so troubling to see the wealth and poverty yoked together in this country. Just off an old two-lane highway in Ecuador, near the school and clinic, there are rich fields that sit in a valley of the cloud forest. The seed scattered in this rich soil yields a hundredfold three or four seasons a year. In those same fields, dirt-poor campesinos (farmers) and concrete shanties are well rooted. We once traveled to a spot just down the road from the community to buy lemongrass and mint. The spot was just a gap in the road, where skinny dogs with ribs you could count from a distance roamed, waiting for a crumb to be dropped by barefoot children. Behind the littered dirt yard, on the other side of a nearly hidden gate, was an arbor path. While we waited for the gardener to pack up the plants we had purchased, a few of us became sidetracked and started wandering down the dreamy, fragrant path.

The path was flanked by a beautiful orchard, heavy with mangoes and cocoa fruit. The orchards sloped downhill, littered with fruit trees for as far as you could see. As we continued walking, I kept thinking about how this path was the epitome of the disparity that tears the world apart. On this path you could see the wealth of a vast orchard before harvest, and just down the road you could see the poverty of children with scabies holding on to starving dogs. The image provided a dramatic illustration of the sickness of the world that lives in me. I feel that tension all the time as I decide how to spend my money and where to lay my head. I was grateful for that side road that helped me look a little closer than just a quick drive along the two-lane highway. The fields of this world are troubled, and when we take the time to sit in them, they can't help but trouble our souls.

The fields of Ecuador call me to rethink my ideas of justice, complacency, and ignorance. These aren't a distraction from my life in Nashville; they are some of the most powerful fields I have known. When I sit in that field and soak in the sunlight with all kinds of concoctions on my body to protect myself from the mosquitoes and glaring sun, I remember that our world is both unjust and lovely. These troubled fields provide an opportunity to back up and remember what I believe and the truth about my life.

A story in the twelfth chapter in John's Gospel describes Jesus walking through the fields of Bethany. The journey seems like a distraction because he's supposed to be walking toward Jerusalem. He backtracks, to the place where he raised his friend, Lazarus, from certain death, and sits for supper. Martha hasn't changed a bit; she's still taking care of everyone as she prepares and serves supper. The whole event seems like a side story as we wait for the triumphal entry into Jerusalem, until we recognize it as a troubled space—one where beautiful lessons on love can be found.

Danger surrounded Jesus. With the opposition and recent death of John the Baptist, Mary decided at dinner to take out her burial oils and anoint Jesus. She poured all the pure-scented nard on his bare feet and opened the most sacred and troubled space where life and death meet. In those tender spaces, lines once drawn in the sand fade with the slightest breeze and blur into love's hold. The side path becomes central in that act, and the oils are a sacramental sign that trouble is present and healing is coming. That moment must have felt like a dream to Mary as pain and sweetness stirred her troubled heart. That dinner in Bethany is a rich and hard field where community and loneliness collide. It's a place where humility meets courage, and lavishness and economics face off. Jesus uses it as a place to help remind everyone of love's axioms.

Judas, in his own troubled state, protests that the oils should have been sold. Those oils, still filling the room with their perfume, become spark for the proclamation that I have come to understand as a great blessing on the journey: "The poor will always be with you."[1] In other words, Jesus is giving us the gift that our fields will always be troubled. We will always get to take side roads that change our hearts as we learn what it means for love to heal.

As we walk a side road on our journey and find ourselves in troubled fields with open hearts, we learn how to love better and what it means to pour out our best oils to soothe suffering. It is our own poverty that enables us to see the richness of compassion. Every year, after we have seen a thousand people in the clinic in Ecuador, we backtrack as we reflect on the week and what we could do to improve the services. We sit in a circle, take a cue from Mary, and use our geranium oils to anoint each other's feet. Doctors, children, well workers, cooks, teachers, painters, and friends kneel down and get a sense of the depth of love that rises from such troubled fields. It's hard to know how in this troubled world we are cutting a straight path through our deserts of hurt. It's hard to know how we can even cut through the mountains and the valleys to make the path easier for those coming after us. It is hard to know in the sweet darkness where true north lies.

Sometimes it feels like the world is too harsh and big for a little jar of oil to help anyway, no matter how fine it is. Sometimes oils aren't helpful, and using them would simply make me a pushy snake oil salesman. Sometimes it feels like using them would be like throwing pearls before swine, and that I have wasted the gift. When I walk around with all those worries and depressing thoughts like "nothing changes" or "I am no good at any of this," I know it's time to go back two steps and remember how healing works and why oils are a part of that process.

Our efforts seem feeble compared to the suffering and problems of the world created by poverty. How do we help individuals in a meaningful way in the midst of a global economic crisis? What does it mean to pour oils on one person when more than three billion people are living in poverty? In comparison with the enormity of the issues, our response to pull out some oil and offer it as a gift seems almost funny. Small deeds in a big world are always humbling. I know that I don't have to make people love me; I just have to love others. But I would rather not humiliate myself while I'm trying to be loving. Sometimes I worry about what I say, how my hair looks, and whether my skin appears old. I know that is not what I am supposed to be thinking about.

The most basic laws of faith are to love God with all our hearts, minds, and souls and to love our neighbors as ourselves. That means to me that I am not supposed to focus on my worries. I am to focus on loving the world. The command is also the tallest order, and it requires our entire lives to fulfill. This is one of the lessons we circle around to better understand.

Once upon a time, to help us when we feel overwhelmed by the enormousness of the task of loving a world laden with burdens, someone wrote a story about a starfish thrower. In the story, a man walks down a beach and sees a little boy bend to pick up a beached starfish, which he then throws back into the ocean to save its life. The passerby questions the thrower about the difference throwing one starfish back could possibly make. Millions of others line the beach. The thrower tosses another back in the ocean and says it makes all the difference to the starfish he just threw back.

The story works on many levels for people who feel lost as they set out to help heal the world. When you read the story from the perspective of the starfish thrower, it is a lifesaving parable about compassion, in which the thrower loves the starfish like himself. From the perspective of the passerby, the story becomes a call to learn the law of love again and how to love specifically. But this sweet story can carry us only so far on the journey to fulfill God's call to love with our whole hearts. It doesn't give us enough insight into the details of how we heal the world with the hands God has given us. The story can seem kind of depressing to those who read it and want to be the one who throws starfish.

You can imagine the thrower walking down the beach and rescuing starfish endlessly, giving the story a layer of loneliness in the monotonous task that lies ahead. He may wonder if he will be throwing starfish while forces more powerful will continue to wash a greater number up on shore. He may dream about quitting, because he can't imagine that this is the sum total of his life. He probably knows his actions mean something to the starfish and the passerby but wonders about the meaning of his own life.

You can substitute starfish throwing with a number of activities of devotion and service. My version of starfish throwing has definitely been my life at Magdalene. I may have begun the work on the right path, but sometimes I feel lost and overwhelmed. Sometimes the work feels like it's barely a drop in the bucket. Recently, I read that the State Department estimates that more than two million people are trafficked annually in this world.[2] According to Shared Hope International, more than one hundred thousand children in the United States between the ages of twelve and eighteen are at risk for sex trafficking each year. They also claim that child pornography is a three-billion-dollar-a-year industry. Just recently at St. Augustine's Chapel, where I serve as chaplain, I met a seventeen-year-old woman in foster care who has been trafficked for years already. In an ocean of addiction and on shores of a culture that tolerates the buying and selling of human beings, we house only twenty-seven women in Nashville, Tennessee.

All I can do is circle back and return to the axioms of love that determine how love heals. I get a closer look every time I begin anew. These principles teach us that if love has no beginning or end, then healing can manifest itself in a way in which the sum is greater than its parts. Moses, the giver of the law, spent forty years lost in the desert as he led his people toward the Promised Land. He kept leading them and climbing Mount Sinai, dreaming of the day he could stop wandering. Toward the end of his life, God calls him to the mountain one last time. He has been faithful for 120 years. Finally God shows him his heart's desire, but then says that he has to die on this side of the Jordan. Moses lies down and dies as God commands.[3] Yet Moses' law, like love itself, lived on and is still the law we write on our children's hearts. His story teaches us that all acts of love live beyond our temporal lives and are part of the great law of eternal love.

The story tells us that acts of love move beyond the service of faithful men and women. Love is not a linear expression; love multiplies exponentially. Love lives beyond our limited vision and is carried by the Spirit into hearts we never know. In faith, the bounty of love is always miraculous and produces visible signs of how love moves. Loving each other is discouraging only when we forget our heritage and need to backtrack to read the summary of Moses' law of love from Deuteronomy again. We miss the depth and breadth of the story of loving one another when we forget all the people who took the time to love us enough to pick us up off the beaches we were stranded on to throw us to safer places. We are not caring for our brothers and sisters out of duty, or for a certain result, but in joyous gratitude for all the people who saved our own lives. We miss the point if we forget the saints who changed the world by loving God, and that loving God, neighbors, and self is a big deed in a small world.

On my small stretch of beach, I discovered the story of Carolyn, a woman who left a violent home in rural Tennessee at the age of thirteen. She was taken to Washington, DC, where she was prostituted on the streets and left for dead. Almost thirty years later she found her way from that barren stretch of beach to the safe shores of Magdalene. Today, she celebrates four years of sobriety and shares her story with church communities and groups. She works full-time at a local coffee shop. She has helped women in prisons, in her family, on the streets, and in congregations to believe that love heals. Imagine Carolyn arm in arm with fellow brothers and sisters, like a huge, long, glorious chain that spans beyond seashores into the mountains and the shadowy valleys. It is a gift to be able to keep walking and to do our part, knowing love will carry us farther than we can imagine, until finally it will carry us back to God. Backsliding and sidetracking, fretting and doubting, can't pull us away from that powerful line.

In a life of faith, backsliding, sidetracking, and backtracking are graceful acts caused by troubled fields, starfish throwing, and the details of one woman's story. Sometimes we trip up and get lost, not just because we were distracted but because we make mistakes. In that space of backsliding, we get to learn and relearn the lesson that love never abandons us. As an axiom, love is sufficient and has no beginning or end. This foundational understanding of love is aided by the fact that the most radical love we can know in the world is love without judgment. So backsliding, even when our actions mean dealing with some hard medicine, like humiliation and failure, can give us some great insight into how love heals.

Backtracking is critical to learning how to love, so learning how to backtrack gracefully is an important skill. It's a skill to learn to say *I've lost my way* or *I have forgotten the point* or *That makes no sense and I don't believe it.*

It is in times and places when we feel troubled and need to do some backtracking that love does its best work. It is in the troubling places where fear is a companion that love keeps us walking. When I am scared and lost, I know I am desperate for a healing word or sign. I am willing to search high and low for any sign of a healing path. In some of the worst places, like the alleys where women I know have been raped, we have found unexpected paths of forgiveness that lead to Gilead. In villages where AIDS has put down such deep roots we have seen love dig deeper. At Thistle Farms, when we feel frustrated and lost as the company grows, we gather and light a candle and return to the truth that love heals, and somehow we find a new path we never knew. It honestly feels like love can lead us round and round until we find ourselves in exactly the right spot.

But we are bound to backslide and even fall sometimes. Ego and self-consciousness can make us all backslide and fall on our backsides every now and then. A good fall lets us be close to the earth, even if our hands and hearts get a little scraped up in the process. At times I've become so preoccupied with what others think about the work I am doing that I have tried to hide failures or exaggerate successes at Magdalene and Thistle Farms. Living like that is exhausting and leaves me feeling like a failure. Especially when someone has relapsed or died, I have worried that people would think that I was incompetent, that the program didn't work, or that we were not worthy of their time, consideration, or support. Consistently over the past two decades I have learned from backsliders that wherever brokenness is present, people will cry with you. You don't have to cover up mistakes for fear of judgment or apologize for a disease you have no control over.

It's not fight or flight in snake oil; it's learning to do the dance in between gracefully. That is why we have to backtrack, get sidetracked, and backslide. We all get a little unfocused and lost. Sometimes I think I have no business even talking about this stuff, let alone trying to sell it. When I stop and remember all the times that I have messed up, gotten mad, or hurt people, I have to remind myself that I am here by grace and people have forgiven me more than I have had to forgive.

I can talk with some ease about the abuse I experienced as a child and about forgiving my abuser, but it's much harder to confess the times when I have used people or things for my own purposes. I hate some of the truth about my life and how far I still need to go. What saves me from slipping into the ditch as I start sliding down the hill is the simple revelation that I am not alone. The problem with shame is that it makes you believe you are alone in this world, and that if the truths about your past or your sin were revealed, you would be abandoned or unloved. I remember my failures. I let them humble me sufficiently. And then I start climbing again. It doesn't serve the community to stay in the pit of unworthiness. It is better for the community for me to remember the miraculous force that is love. Love comes in and dusts off our knees. Love whispers in our ears to remind us that it is stronger than the memories or past deeds that can cripple us on our journey. Love is what calls from the depths of the earth to experience a deeper truth. Love diminishes sin and death and upholds anyone who wants to walk toward it.

Being sidetracked is usually an adventure. I was passing through a small town called Manchester in the foothills of Tennessee and got sidetracked by a sign advertising the Arrowheads to Aerospace Museum. If the title doesn't pull you in, then the promise of train rides and buttons at least makes your head cock to one side like a curious dog. As it turns out, it's a museum focused on preserving Southern culture from the time of the Civil War up to the beginning of the civil rights movement. The displays begin with a single arrowhead display collected from the surrounding creeks, then jump to memorabilia from the Civil War. More displays feature life for white Southerners from around the turn of the twentieth century up until the end of the 1950s.

The curator explained that they stopped in the 1950s because that is when they built the plant nearby that specialized in aerospace technology. In the back corner we saw an apothecary filled with a hundred or so old bottles half-full of liquid. The containers held everything from rhubarb tonic to promises of healing from pain and digestion trouble. Each listed alcohol by at least twenty percent volume. All of these tonics were offered during Prohibition. They had to mix alcohol with herbs and call it snake oil in order to have a drink to take the edge off. Even though the museum felt overtly racist, it was a sign to see the snake oils in the museum's corner as they took their rightful place on the fringe of life, keeping it spirited and a little more honest. The journey into the Arrowheads to Aerospace Museum was a strange and memorable sidetrack. In the end, being sidetracked is usually right on target. In going around the long way, we find the teachings we need to take the next step.

While we humans are good at letting ourselves become sidetracked, life itself can sometimes set us off course. The Middle Tennessee region experienced this in May 2010 when we had the worst flood in our history. There was more than one billion dollars in damage, and we grieved twenty-one deaths. Thousands of homes were damaged by waters that forgot the rivers' boundaries and came pouring into basements and first floors. Fortunately, only one of the six residents of Magdalene was flooded, and Thistle Farms didn't have a drop of water come in even though that neighborhood was one of the hardest hit in the whole city.

I could drive down any street and see piles of moldy discarded carpet, drywall, furnishings, and household goods in front yards. Without garbage pick-up systems in place for the first few weeks, the piles of water-soaked refuse just sat there. As I drove, I subconsciously started measuring neighbors' tragedies by the size of the pile in their front yards. A small pile meant that they were lucky; a big pile meant they had it bad. Some piles were bigger than the ranch-style homes they came from.

St. Augustine's organist's experience of the flood made him backtrack all the way to his beginning. He has his PhD in music and is an avid collector of beautiful music who knows the history of each song. He had been collecting sheet music for more than forty years. His entire apartment was underwater, and he was left with just the clothes on his back. Grieving and in shock, he felt like a phoenix rising from the ashes. There was nothing left, but he had community and love, and that was plenty with which to start over. It was a setback, but it wasn't the same as just starting out. This time he had a whole community of people to rely on, and he had a wealth of experience to draw upon. He had years of prayer and service that gave him wisdom and devotion for the rebuilding. The beginning of this part of his life was also the ending of too much of what he had claimed as his own. As his friend, I found that watching his journey was difficult but inspiring. Months later he found a new home. He says it is his dream place and that he never would have found it if his apartment hadn't flooded, and he swears he has enough gratitude to carry him for miles.

Eventually, by traveling through all the backtracking, backslides, and sidetracks, we see the journey toward holy, sacred ground. Events offer us sacred nuggets of truth and mercy that carry us along the path and are as valuable as gold. They give us the experiences we need to find our voice and then tell our truth. They offer us compassion for all that others have gone through and the chance to be better healers.

Chapter Ten

LAUGHING IN
THE WIND

Balm of Joy

4 ounces aloe vera oil
10 drops bergamot essential oil
10 drops lotus essential oil
16 drops grapefruit essential oil
2 drops champa essential oil

Combine all of the ingredients. The champa
is sweet, sensual, and floral. The lotus is
exotic. Grinding these with the happy scents
of grapefruit and bergamot results in a joyful
oil that's good for the body. Use on your skin
or in your bath. Balm of Joy is good for your
immune system and brings balance to you
when you feel stressed. You can strengthen
or weaken the oil by adding or deleting the

amount of essential oil. This is a good oil to use even when a blue sky seems a little dreary.

THE FIRST TIME I met Doris her teeth and hair showed the signs of years of neglect. She was very self-conscious and seemed shy to me. But after months of hard work on her part and by the community, Doris's new teeth shine as she laughs, and her hair is cropped in a soft afro that halos her radiant face. Doris is a joyful employee of Thistle Farms who says that she can do anything because she was given 9,450 days of grace in her life. She arrived at that number by calculating how long she survived on the streets.

When you find your way down into the packing department on the basement level at Thistle Farms, sometimes you can hear Doris singing before you see her. When you do see her in this tucked-away area of Thistle Farms, she will probably be dressed in a long dress that allows her beauty to shine. She has a contagious smile.

I have heard Doris talk with incredible dignity about watching her father die when she was nine. As she told the story, she described the aftershocks that can still send her tumbling forty-five years later.

I traveled with her to a small liberal arts college in Pennsylvania. We went to talk to the nursing students, the religion majors, and the business school. Doris had never flown before and came to the airport dressed to the nines with a fur purse, beaded shoes, and a brown pashmina over a leopard-patterned top and pants. She took pictures and posted them to Facebook before she even stepped foot in the airport.

As soon as the plane started down the runway for take-off she started laughing. She provided the clearest and most compelling example of laughing in the wind that I've ever seen. Her laughter made all the other passengers around her smile. The laughter contained a blend of excitement, fear, and wonder. As we picked up speed and started to lift off she just said, "Oh, my Lord," repeatedly and just laughed and laughed. She took out her phone as soon as we started ascending, and I didn't have the heart to tell her she was not supposed to turn it on. Instead I watched her in wonder take a picture of a lake and clouds from the topside for the first time. She fired questions at me about the magic of flight and then asked me, "Is this as close to God as I will ever be until I die?" and then laughed. It brought tears to my eyes as I said, "Sometimes when I am with you, Doris, it feels as close to God as I can get." Laughter and tears feel to me like they are born out of the same place. They are cousins rooted in the heart. They both overflow and keep me going forward on this path.

Van Morrison titled one of his classic hits "Laughing in the Wind." In the song, he says that laughing in the wind is like crying in the rain. Those kinds of classic rock lyrics provide a background to growing up in the seventies. They still pop into my head when I mean to quote scripture or think of a theological way to explain something. To me, laughing in the wind is the opposite of whining. The phrase doesn't indicate that life is pointless, but instead signifies our need to surrender to laughter found in the wind itself. Laughing in the wind is like joining the chorus of laughter found in the wind itself. The wind doesn't care if we laugh or not, so we laugh because we want to. It doesn't matter if another soul hears the laughter. We laugh for the sake of laughing.

My mother was the best at laughing in the wind. So much is forgiven and forgotten in death as time is marked in years. What stays with me are memories and lessons ingrained from watching how she moved in this world. As so much fades, what I remember about her most is her laughter. She had a wide and easy smile and would break into laughter with little provocation. My mother loved jokes, and she especially loved what I think has been one of my saving graces—macabre humor. Even in pretty dark and hard times, she would find something funny and that would become part of the story. Laughter helps heal what ails you. A sense of humor helps get you through what otherwise might be some pretty long days.

One of my distinct memories of my father's funeral was the ninety-minute ride to the burial site on Sewanee Mountain. We piled into a car, and all I could think about was that it was going to be a long ride. Dad had died only two days earlier, and I was tired. A long line of cars made the journey with us, and we were in the front car, right behind the hearse. About twenty minutes into the ride I said to my sister, "I know a joke." When she told me that this was not the time to tell jokes, my mom, who was sitting in the front seat beside the driver, turned and said, "I'd love to hear your joke." I don't remember what I said, although I am fairly certain it probably was neither funny nor appropriate, but my family laughed with me, and I was grateful that it was okay to be funny even when your father is dead and you have to spend all day driving to bury him. Laughing in the midst of grieving is a necessary and beautiful gift.

Laughing in the wind is a special kind of laughter. Rather than just laughing aloud, this kind of laughter is more of a surrendering with an unspoken assurance that even if we fall, love will catch us. Such laughter doesn't come from joke telling or contrived stories, but bubbles up from a deep place of brokenness and sometimes from a surrender of the "What the hell?" sort.

Thirty-five years later I was in those same hills of Tennessee where we buried my father, preaching about Thistle Farms at a small Episcopal church. I told them the story of how I named the company after the thistle, which has a history of survival by brutality and a soft, beautiful purple center. I told them that the closest I have ever come to laughing in the wind was when I realized that I had become a thistle farmer years and years after naming the company. It felt like I was becoming the theology I was professing to others. I was both humbled and refreshed by the transformation.

Being in the field plucking thistles signaled the actual beginning of my becoming a bona fide snake oil seller. I'm so grateful that I didn't miss the thistle fields and wild oils in the world. I am so grateful that by chance we picked the one weed in the world of weeds that has been used for more than a thousand years to restore and detoxify the liver. It is a miracle given that Thistle Farms serves many women who are hepatitis C positive and suffer liver disease from extensive drug and alcohol abuse. Without knowing it, the women of Magdalene had been picking it, soaking in it, and letting the oils from the plant be absorbed into their skin as they pressed thistle paper. I learned later that the thistle essence is recommended when a person needs to overcome great hardship and trauma. The history of the thistle is a confirmation that we are drawn toward the healing we need.

I wanted to inspire the folks in that small church that healing is possible for us all and that the new information on how thistles heal livers was confirmation for me. I felt like I had preached a refreshing message to people who didn't hear these kinds of stories or give much thought to the thistle.

After the service I walked out onto the small path in front of the church and greeted folks. An older woman took me down the path to an old stone archway. Above the path in big block letters carved some hundred years before was: SHE PLUCKED THE THISTLE AND PLANTED A FLOWER. The statement made me laugh and set me gently back in my place. Making healing oils and sharing them with the world is nothing new. It is as old as the hills I was preaching in. What is new is the inspiration we feel as we walk the old path of faith. Walking into the huge problems in our world, like a thistle farmer, seems like laughing in the wind, but it also seems like walking into the world with an unguarded heart is one of the most powerful ways love heals. Who are we to believe we can soothe the suffering, heal the brokenhearted, and help restore lives? We are people willing to laugh in the wind and join in a chorus of people who hope and find joy in the journey itself.

My family are all longtime recreational fishermen, and we were completely skunked on a recent trip to Florida. It was billed as a rich and varied fishing expedition, but we didn't see any wildlife except for a flock of seagulls that had caught a nice draft and were making an upward circle near the boat and cackling as they were heading out. "We call those laughing seagulls," the captain of the boat said. Their laughing in the wind sounded like the birds were making fun of us out in the boat casting and casting in waters that held nothing but more water. Their laugh was contagious, and I loved to think that I could join in a chorus of birds literally laughing in the wind.

One morning, we rented kayaks to paddle the beautiful wetlands of the Everglades. As we paddled through the soft light of sunrise, swallowtail kites perched on high branches, preparing to hunt for breakfast. As the sun rose like the eternal phoenix, the temperature rose, and moving through the murky water provided plenty of time to think and reflect. The Everglades contain countless gifts. The red mangrove trees thrive in this area because they are one of the few species of tree that can survive salt water.

Red mangroves have a massive root system that reaches two feet above the water's surface. The root system acts like a huge filter to prevent the salt from going up into the tree. By the time the water reaches the trunk, it is purified and only a little salt remains. The mangrove diverts all the salt into certain leaves called sacrificial leaves that take in the salt, turn yellow, and return to the water. In the water, the smallest animals eat the leaves, and thus the mangrove is central to the whole Everglades ecosystem. This red mangrove, with its yellow sacrificial leaves, is a symbol of how everything on the journey can be used for healing. The plant is a tender symbol for the way we offer our gifts to each other for the collective healing of all.

The mangrove reminds me that it is okay to laugh at some of the hardest and saddest things. God knows it's hard enough, and our laughter is like the massive root system that filters out some of the salt water of tears. Laughter is good medicine. We, like red mangrove trees, heal when we shoot the salty sediments toward leaves that we then shed. We let go those parts of ourselves—those yellow leaves—so that the whole system can be nourished.

We cannot go into the salty waters made up of sweat and tears to love the world without being able to laugh. The joyous expression of laughter helps us grow, filter, and feed our spirits. If anybody thinks that they can take it all in without laughing some of it off, they will drown in tears. At times, life is too hard and too sad. When I hear stories of young women watching their sisters being raped or having to sleep in the bathtub because it's the only safe place or watching their daddy die, I cry. And more often than not, somewhere along the journey, we all will laugh about funny and morose stuff. It's good to shed a few leaves as we grow new ones.

Like the shedding of salty leaves, laughter gives us a sign that we are open to change on our journey. The laughter and tears are both signs to me that it's time to cleanse, laugh, grow, and heal. All of us have those moments when we can laugh and cry and feel our lives shifting a bit. We can all think back to those moments: *This part no longer fits. This part of my life has to take in the salt, and I have to let it go.*

At the end of our journey in Florida, my family returned home. I was scheduled to travel to New York to meet with the board of a chain of natural food stores to talk about the future of Thistle Farms. For the past several years, we had known that we needed the support of a large chain and a new facility in order to maintain the work of our thirty-five employees.

The conversation about how to approach a big retailer as a vendor was the beginning of a major shift in my thinking. Instead of being a sweet local charity for a few women, we were going to be seen as a national company. It was time for us to become a stronger voice and to take this dream to the next level. Getting a big account would enable Thistle Farms to become a brand we could market and use to support the residential communities. We needed to shed some leaves, laugh, and cry a bit.

I felt knots in my stomach because I knew that without this work, the women at Thistle Farms would never be able to reach economic independence or even pay to fix a flat tire without undue stress. We knew we could manufacture three times more and speak to many more groups and maybe help reshape a world that still buys and sells women. We wanted to stand up to human trafficking and speak our truth in love. We wanted to talk about the consequences of child sexual abuse on people's bodies and in their lives. We could help people make a sustainable living, but we needed the help of a major chain. We had preached, talked, and dreamed about it a lot. The plan was written. Now it was time to go to New York to have the meeting.

I felt nauseous the morning of the meeting. Dreaming and talking about the proposal was fun, but I didn't want to present it. I was afraid of messing up, and I was afraid of what it would take to triple our business in a year. The first thing I saw when I checked my email that morning was a message that said, "We're all praying for you," which is usually a sweet thing, but that morning it just made me more nervous. I could imagine all the women sitting at Thistle Farms, saying a prayer, and I was about to mess everything up. I feared saying something inappropriate and being rejected by the daunting professionals I was trying to impress. I did not want to shed a leaf that day. I hate the taste of salt. I thought, *I cannot fight this. This is bigger than me. I do not want this change. I like the way I've been living.*

I spent the morning nervously wandering the streets of New York with eight million other people, waiting for the three o'clock meeting. I wandered until I found myself in between two buildings at a little gated space—a small cemetery. I could not make out the writing on a single stone. A plaque explained that the cemetery held a group of Jewish Portuguese immigrants who came to New York in the 1820s. As I looked at that cemetery, I saw a beautiful, quiet place where everything was laid to rest. I felt like I was witnessing where transformation is complete. In that graveyard, I couldn't make out individual names anymore. Successes and failures—all the things we hold on to—make no difference. All return to God. I felt so much freedom in that space. I felt freed to be just a child of God, completely open to love, and whatever happened next, it would be a great gift.

The vision of the cemetery at peace was akin to laughing in the wind. Both are a surrender to the truth and the futility of life sometimes. When we surrender to that, we are completely free. After the journey into the cemetery, I headed to my meeting and took the elevator to the top floor, where the head of the company was gracious and loving and listened to our story. He committed to working with Thistle Farms so that our products could be carried in all their stores.

I was thrilled that the work and dedication of the women at Thistle Farms had paid off, but I knew something else mattered more. I was learning again that our faith will change us. All of us need to be continually transformed and freed from ourselves, from all of our fears and all of the things we worry about that prevent us from fully loving the world. We get to walk around as optimistic and hopeful as we want to be. We are like a red mangrove, taking in the salt, shedding the excess, and growing so we can go back out and love the world, again and again.

Laughing in the wind is the idea of surrendering in mind, body, and spirit to where love leads. In letting go and going where the winds of love carry you, you will find yourself. Some of the great and courageous stories of people who laughed in the wind and tried to make a difference in the world have these moments of letting go. They have surrendered to their work—a laughing in the wind of sorts.

Early on in Dorothy Day's ministry, when she started the Catholic Worker Movement, she described how one day while she was out on the streets selling the *Catholic Worker* newspaper, she walked by a church and stopped. She said that she just couldn't pass it by. She talked about how from that day standing in front of that church her passion for justice was inextricably linked to her search for God, and she was transformed by the search. For Dorothy Day and many other healers and seekers, it seems like they can pinpoint the moment that things are going to be different.

I remember laughing in the wind one sweltering July day the year after the first house had opened. There was enough money on the books at Magdalene to last only another few weeks; summer is the lean season for not-for-profits. Money is the issue that sends me into fear and doubt faster than just about anything. I worry that the money won't be there and the houses will shut down and the whole venture will end. It is a familiar companion on my path. While I was fretting about money, Regina, one of the first residents, called to ask me about bringing an old friend into the house. "But the house is full," I said.

"I know, but this is my friend Lisa," Regina said. "And I know you have access to another house over on Arthur Street."

The house she mentioned had been donated to St. Luke's community center when my mom still ran it. Since then the home had been given to another organization, but they had said we could use it when we were ready. The question was whether or not I wanted to double our burden when money was tightest, or to tell Lisa that there was nowhere for her to live. Regina already knew the answer before she called. When I said, "Okay, but I am really nervous," Lisa was already packed and ready to go. It made me laugh—what else can you do? I was laughing because it was a natural response to surrendering to a calling in which you feel like you are just along for the ride.

It's important to be able to laugh in the wind when you sell snake oils, because folks will sometimes just roll their eyes when you talk about the "amazing qualities" of your oils. No matter how much you know or how much evidence you present, some people will always be skeptical.

In the realm of snake oils, you have to see the world a little differently. Where others see poverty, you see riches; where others see weeds, you see flowers; where others see sickness, you see openness. All of that makes dealing in snake oils a heroic and noble trade. Snake oil salesmen carry around healing oils for sale and find themselves coming to terms with the most vulnerable parts of people's lives.

Most people lead with their strength, but if they believe you can help ease their pain, people will show you their weak spots. It is a privilege to get to hold a broken arm or touch fresh scars. It seems so clear that God enters our lives most easily in those places—not in our times of great strength and confidence, but when we realize we are unsure and need help. Those moments of clarity and inspiration are more fleeting to me than I like to think sometimes.

The work of making and selling oils can often make a person feel like Sisyphus rolling his stone uphill. For about six months after we got our products into the chain, I spent Monday and Wednesday mornings making healing oil boxes at Thistle Farms with four or five other women. On Tuesdays and Thursdays, I drove out to the local health food store that was part of the national chain that was carrying our products and bought one or two things to help drive sales. I laughed in the wind a few times on those drives. It felt like buying those products just might be the drop in the bucket that would make the bucket of sales overflow. I was hoping that those small sales might trigger other stores in the chain to place big orders too. We made the products, and then I drove twenty miles to buy them back at retail.

The work was akin to going grocery shopping, cooking

all the food, putting it on plates, and then scraping it all off when your kids say they're not hungry. It's like going running before I pick up my kids and then deciding to stop at the ice cream shop on the way home. It might be better to skip the whole process, except that the process, when done in love, completely changes us, and we find we are richer for the journey. Because I was buying the Thistle Farms products, I decided that I should start using them more. I started bathing with them again and letting all the oils soak in. I had forgotten how rich they are and how good they smell and feel. I had forgotten that they are meant for my healing and not just for others'. On some level that realization may have saved my sanity or even helped the company grow.

Dealing in oils reminds me how unbelievably rich I am and how, as long as I always serve, I will be free. The oils remind me to keep looking at the world from the alleys, prisons, and lonely paths to get a better perspective. They remind me to not take anything but love too seriously. Sometimes in the late summer, when the purple thistles turn white and we enter the drought season of fund-raising, I watch the white down of a thistle blow in the wind. I swear it looks like laughing. Those downy seeds in the wind are symbols of how we can live more freely by laughing in the wind than by holding on to our fears. Laughing in the wind is transformational and allows us to keep moving along down the path of healing.

Chapter Eleven

THE FRAGRANCE
OF HEALING

An Aromatic Oil

1 ounce aloe vera oil
1 ounce sweet almond oil
8 drops rose oil
8 drops sweet orange essential oil
4 drops patchouli essential oil

Pour all of the ingredients into a glass
container and whisk to combine. Enjoy at
bath time. Just pour a couple of capfuls into
the water and breathe. At the heart of this
recipe is the rose, one of my favorite scents,
which is perfect for a bath. If you have another
floral scent that is your favorite, you can
substitute it for the rose. Although it's not a
decongestant, this rich floral scent will enrich

your spirit. Don't be surprised if it carries you to the past and lets you enjoy a memory you haven't thought about in a long, long time.

ONE OF THE GREAT gifts of being a part of the Thistle Farms enterprise is getting to research and purchase new essential oils. The goal is for everyone to play with the new blends that we might use in our products. The process begins with someone having an idea for a new scent that we want to make, like lemon-sage, and then asking our research and development team to order a few ounces of the essential oils. Then we gather the company together for a day to play with fragrance. Everyone is invited to participate.

In addition to the new scent, the research and development team brings out other essential oils that people might want to add to enhance the fragrance. We also play with which carrier oil (such as almond oil or olive oil) works best. Then we label all the samples people have made and everyone takes their time deciding and voting for their top three. By the end of a couple days, it's pretty clear which fragrances are the favorites. We offer these top scents to the research and development team to refine and develop into products. Being a part of the making of the fragrance makes the end product even more special. Now when I smell our lemon-sage candle, I inhale a history and remember that fun day when we all stopped production and played with lemon and sage.

Being a part of the preparation and presentation is a great joy in the making of healing oils. As Gwen talked to us about the uses of lemon and sage, the aroma filled the room. As I sat across the table from Gwen and Chelle, who were mixing their lemon-sage into fragrant apricot oil, we caught up with each other and shared stories about our kids. Making the oils not only changed the ions in the room, it also reopened our hearts to one another.

Usually when I make oils I get caught up in the fragrance. It might trigger the lesson from an old wives' tale that teaches me to stir the oil counterclockwise because it is toward your heart. When I make oils, I love to use the same wooden spoon and write notes about where the individual oils came from. If we are part of the planting of the plants, the distilling of the oils from the leaves, and the prayers that are offered as they are made, we breathe in the gift of the oils during every stage. As we make the oils, we get to smell the lavender in the field as the buds are shaken, as the oil heats, and when the tincture is poured on skin. Being a part of the creation becomes part of the healing process.

Learning to make our own concoctions combines creativity and purposefulness. For Thistle Farms to grow into manufacturing oils for the concoctions, balms, and oils, we realized we would need a still. Though they are best known for their use in making whiskey, stills have been used for hundreds of years to distill the essence of fruits, vegetables, and plants through a heating and cooling process. A still consists of a large vat that holds the plant. Underneath the still you fire up a heat source that boils the water inside the airtight vat. Once the water boils, its steam heats the plant. The steam from the water and the heated plant rise in an

airtight system that flows into a copper tube that is surrounded by cool water. As the steam cools, it condenses into
oil and water. Then the oil and water separate and are collected in two separate glass beakers. The only problem is
that stainless steel stills are expensive.

Last year I spoke to a women's club about our dream
of owning a still. The next day I was leaving for Africa
for a month. To be completely honest, I would have can-
celed except that my friend Joanne had asked me to speak
to the club. When I finished speaking, Joanne's daughter,
Cathy, approached me and said she wanted to present Thistle
Farms with the still in her mother's honor. Her mother loved
the work we did at Thistle Farms, and the gift would be
a great surprise of honor. Joanne was losing her sight and
had been a very gifted gardener. If we had the still and we
used her flowers, she could still enjoy the flowers through
the aroma of the oil. Less than three months later we held
a surprise party for Joanne at Thistle Farms at which we
dedicated the still and celebrated our new ability to take our
own plants, such as sage and lavender, and turn them into
healing oils. The alchemy of the still itself is a healing journey.

Before the gift of this still, we had to order all our
essential oils online. We still order many of our oils, but
the still gives the company an opportunity to partner with
other groups interested in growing organic herbs that we
can purchase locally. It also provides two additional jobs.

While stills have traditionally been used to make alcohol
that can keep addicts sick, at Thistle Farms we use one as a
tool to make healing products. The irony is not lost on us.

Entering the manufacturing space while the still is brewing lavender is like being overcome by an aromatic wave of peace and joy.

The first woman hired to run the still is a resident of Magdalene named Jennifer. Jennifer is the youngest of twelve children whose father used physical abuse as a form of discipline. Sexual abuse by an older relative began early. By the time she was in high school, she was a runaway and involved in drugs. During her long journey, Jennifer's drug use escalated to include cocaine and heroin, and that led to street prostitution. At her lowest point she remembers her ex-husband putting her head through a glass window after a heated fight. Jennifer knew she had to find a better way of life. She came to Magdalene at the recommendation of a Catholic priest in her home state in the Midwest. She is a joyful person who sings while she works and offers visitors smells of the various lemongrass and lavender oils she creates. She said it is no accident that she is the lead oil maker, because her advice to women just coming in is "Take a deep breath, relax, and know this is the first day of the rest of your life."

The importance of fragrance cannot be overestimated. The world is never void of fragrance. Even sterilized environments have an odor. The smell of the oils is the first thing people comment on when they walk through the doors at Thistle Farms. People feel strengthened and hopeful just walking through the entrance hall.

Fragrance doesn't make us immortal, but it does bring

us into the presence of the eternal. Fragrance carries us faster than anything to the past. Pleasant scents bring us into the present and free us to dream of the future. Fragrance accompanies the dead to the grave, fills sanctuaries, and is poured over everything we love.

Entire tomes are dedicated to explaining all the ways in which fragrance works on our mental, physiological, and spiritual health. When you are out of balance, spraying geranium and juniper drops mixed in distilled water over your face can dissolve tension. When you are stressed, a few drops of lavender on an eye pillow and breathing deeply for ten minutes can bring you back into a more peaceful state. Distilled ginger oil with aloe vera oil rubbed into your back helps to ease pain. When we apply the art of aromatherapy with snake oils, our world is a better and richer place.

I hiked on the northwest Olympic Peninsula last summer with my husband and three sons. It was pretty early in the morning, and there were wildflowers growing through the snow. The combination of wildflowers and fresh snow was a new scent for me. I don't have the exact words for it, but it's wet and clear at the same time. As we walked along the ridge through the Indian paints and lupine, I was filled with peace. The fragrance of flowers in snow filled my mind with visions of travelers for a thousand years crossing this ridge and breathing in this sight. I was content to breathe in the smell and let this new memory wash over me. It conjured up hundreds of images for me and I traveled through time. Visions come easily with a new fragrance that takes us to the mountaintop.

Fragrance feels like a living prayer that carries us to the edge of time itself. I can recall the sweet smell of the river and am transported to the bank, where I see my sons running and laughing and daring each other to dive again into the frigid river water. Fragrance doesn't hold us to a certain age or location but instead frees us to float with thoughts through windows of memory and imagination. Fragrance is a path toward freedom.

The smell of a hospital or nursing home stirs strong memories and feelings in me. The last time I visited a veteran on the locked Alzheimer's ward, the scent of urine mixed with antiseptic hit me, and I began to cry. The smell translated to abandonment mixed with my own fear of getting old. Other hospital smells are not nearly as haunting, but the smells that hit me as I walk in a veterans' nursing home bring to the forefront of my mind the fleeting gift of health and memory.

Hospitals are good places to bring sweet fragrances. When my friend Francis was dying at the hospital, his family called me to come and offer the prayers. In the Episcopal tradition, it's customary to carry anointing oils to those who are dying and offer these old and beautiful words from the Book of Common Prayer:

Almighty God, look on this your servant, lying in great weakness, and comfort him with the promise of life everlasting, given in the resurrection of your Son Jesus Christ our Lord. Amen.

Depart, O Christian soul, out of this world; In the name of God the Father Almighty who created you; In the name of Jesus Christ who redeemed you; In the name of the Holy Spirit who sanctifies you. May your rest be this day in peace, and your dwelling place in the Paradise of God.

Into your hands, O merciful Savior, we commend your servant. Acknowledge, we humbly beseech you, a sheep of your own fold, a lamb of your own flock, a sinner of your own redeeming. Receive him into the arms of your mercy, into the blessed rest of everlasting peace, and into the glorious company of the saints in light. Amen.

May his soul and the souls of all the departed, through the mercy of God, rest in peace. Amen.[1]

The oils I carried into that hospital room were an old blend of cinnamon, clove, and olive oils. Francis's wife, Becky, used the same oils a few months before during our church's annual pilgrimage to Ecuador. On the annual trip we set up a health clinic during the days but always spend time in the evening in reflection. She had been in that circle just a few months before, so imagine how the scent of those oils carried her right to that circle, bringing her comfort and hope.

When I came in the room, we all gathered around Francis's bed and began by reading Psalm 131:

O LORD, I am not proud;
I have no haughty looks.

I do not occupy myself with great matters,
or with things that are too hard for me.
But I still my soul and make it quiet,
like a child upon its mother's breast;
my soul is quieted within me.
O Israel, wait upon the LORD,
from this time forth for evermore.

Then I read the prayer for the dying from the Book of Common Prayer and opened the oils to anoint his head and feet. Francis was bound with tubes and machines and he had IVs in both arms, but I could still touch his tender head and feet. When I finished, Becky asked if I would place some of the oil on her wrists. Then, she took the oils from me and offered them to her younger sister. Soon everyone in the room was touched by the oil. Meanwhile, Becky told stories about how we used the oils in Ecuador and how they filled the old church we used as a clinic with a holy aroma. The scent of the oils did the same thing in Francis's room, filling the room with a peace that passes understanding. When the nurse returned, she asked Becky if she could have some oil too. Becky anointed the nurse's wrists. The oils were neither scary nor unfamiliar. They were like old friends that brought intimacy and comfort to a group of people who were grieving.

Francis died soon after. After they removed the equipment from his body, we were able to anoint him one last time, and the oils blended with tears as Becky let Francis go. Even in his death the scent of love filled the room. Oils are a wonderful part of our joy and sorrow, beloved tools in my old medicine box. When I use them I feel like my mother's daughter, using whatever I have for the sake of healing. When I use them I feel like a disciple of Jesus, who in the face of pain uses what gifts are available while praying that it is blessed.

The experience of being with Francis and his family at his death strengthens my faith. It reminds me of how connected we are to God and that nothing can shake us. But I don't always feel that assured. Sometimes I get scared and undone by death. The stench is overwhelming and debilitating. Sometimes we face it head-on with no background music or special lighting, and it knocks the wind right out of us.

To this day, I carry oils with gratitude for all the gifts of creation that help us find our way home to God. I carry them unashamed of the cynicism that it evokes in others. I carry them along with my car keys and ID in my backpack. I carry them in a small silver vial that I found in an old communion kit.

I used to carry oils in an antique pyx, a small gold case with an embossed silver cross given to me by the daughter of an army chaplain. I had worked with him after his retirement from the service while he was a chaplain at Vanderbilt. A pyx is often used to hold reserved sacraments, but when lined with lamb's wool, the container holds vials of fragrance oils beautifully. The old pyx was used to soothe people in fields of war external and internal for almost forty years. I gave it to a young midwife named Ali, who will fill birth rooms with beautiful fragrances. She is a gifted healer who loves oils and will teach many new mothers how to love oils too. The fragrance of oils is a meaningful way to say goodbye and a lovely way of welcoming new life. I hope that all the lingering prayers that traveled with this pyx for fifty years mix with the new fragrances of life and continue a healing path.

Several years ago, I was walking in that small town in Ecuador. The town was empty, maybe because the residents were out gathering fishing nets or working in the fields. A big church on the street drew my attention because two huge buzzards were perched on the cross atop the steeple. The smell was a mix of sweat and dust. Silence filled the pungent air, and I felt like I needed to see inside the church, which looked abandoned. The thick, arched wooden front doors were locked with heavy chains. All the glassless windows were closed off with wrought iron bars, so the best I could do was hold on to the cold bars and peer into the unlit chancel.

The only one left in the church was Jesus, hanging life-size on the cross above the altar. He appeared to have been hanging there for a hundred years. At first glance, with its buzzards, locked doors, and dusty old crucifixes, the whole scene looked like death incarnate. I thought of Francis, and then a flood of memories of all the people I loved who had died came over me. I wondered, *What if death has the last word and love dies?* Fear overcame me.

Death is powerful and as ominous and foreboding as

buzzards on a steeple. Death seems like it seals the stone over the tomb and kills that which we hold most dear. That church looked like death and symbolized places in my world that feel hopeless. Places filled with the stench of death, like the garbage dump I had driven past to get to this town, even the old horse stall from my childhood. That old horse stall still scares me, as do places like prisons, where institutional depression thrives. It's like the smell of the old flowers laid out in a pile over a grave after the mourners have gone. When we face death up close, nothing that was left unsaid can be said. All most of us can do is just stand there and breathe it in.

Death is present in the midst of life, and it returns at unexpected turns on roads we travel alone. Death packs a pretty hard punch despite Paul's conviction that it has lost its sting. Standing in front of that abandoned church and letting the aura of death fill the mind with the possibility that it might have the last word would have knocked the breath out of anyone.

When I looked again through the barred windows under the buzzards' perch, I could see something else. A series of small square cloths hung across the front of the church and had been painted with suns, trees, and flowers by children; the string of prayers laid out the sweet, deep desires of hearts that know love and hope. A vase of flowers was placed in front of the reserved sacrament. A dove's nest sat on the rafter in the space between the tin roof and concrete wall. Death didn't begin to have the last word. I just had to look again without fear clouding my sight. This was holy ground, I remembered, as I breathed in the fragrance of healing that comes like the finish of a fine red wine. I looked up as the buzzards caught an upward draft and ascended. Francis was going to be healed on this journey, even in his death.

Love has the last word. Buzzards on a cross aren't the sign of death; they are just two angels standing by an empty tomb. Even when we make the grave our bed, we can go down singing "Alleluia, Alleluia, Alleluia!" and catch an almost imperceptible draft as we soar to be with our God. It is a good thing to carry oils to the people we love who are dying; they help us see that love lives beyond the grave. Francis died saying, "This is just the beginning," and it filled all of us who loved him with hope.

At about the same time as Francis's death, Thistle Farms made a commitment to visit ten women's prisons across the country to share the story of hope and healing with women who were incarcerated. I remember thinking that if Thistle Farms wanted to be a healing community, no matter how busy we were in our daily tasks, we needed to go into all the prisons we could and see what was happening and hear the stories of the women inside.

Something is very wrong with our penal system. More than two and a half million people are imprisoned in the United States—the largest number of people imprisoned in any country in the world. Legislatures enforce the thinking that longer prison sentences are the answer for women who have committed nonviolent drug-related crimes. Upon release, a woman is in an even more precarious situation than before—further endangering herself, the community, and costing everyone even more.

Longer sentencing is an ineffective tool in a community that is fearful. Many of the women in Magdalene had experienced the underside of bridges, the backside of cruelty, and the short side of justice long before they experienced the inside of a prison. Our system tightens the cuffs and keeps them there until scars form over the wounds. This unjust system survives because of a disproportionally large percentage of poor women.

I traveled with a group of women to Houston on the eighth stop of our ten-prison tour and carried copies of our book *Find Your Way Home* inscribed a few weeks beforehand by friends of Thistle Farms.[2] We traveled fifty miles outside of Houston to a prison in Dayton, Texas. The women work in big turnip fields in white long-sleeved shirts and pants as officers on horseback watch over them. Then the women head back into their cells, where there is no air-conditioning.

We passed out the books, and I was glad to just sit and watch the program unfold. The women from Thistle Farms spoke, and the musicians sang about hope. A woman from the prison sitting next to me had the book pressed over her face and whispered, "Your books smell so good. You would be surprised; it's the little things that make such a big difference."

Fragrance can transform and heal us. The books were all inscribed with a message of hope, and by coincidence were packed with a few vials of geranium oil that leaked onto the pages. That same fragrance had traveled from Rwanda, where a cooperative of women who have survived genocide went out and worked in fields every day to harvest geranium. It then traveled to Nashville, where we work every day to make healing products for our bodies, minds, and spirits. The books transported that wonderful fragrance through the prison walls to a woman in Houston who breathed in healing.

The fragrance of healing is carried around the world in unexpected places, but it's our loss if we don't stop and smell it. It's our loss if we travel through India and don't breathe in the rich aromas of tuberose and jasmine. It's our loss if we move through Mideast markets and forget to let nutmeg and apple tobacco fill our imaginations with a thousand nights of dreams.

This world is plenty tough enough to tear any of us apart. It can make us run from prison and death and abandoned churches, but in all those places, the fragrance of healing can fill the space with love and hope. It's more than just stopping to smell the roses; it's breathing in grace to remember God's healing power in love. So we carry the fragrances into veterans' nursing homes, hospitals, and prisons, and we breathe. We trust that, in the scale of love, a drop of oil is enough. We walk through our lives and catch a whiff of our childhood by the side of a river and are given the gift of traveling back to receive healing. Fragrance reminds us not to be too tied to linear time on the path; it's more of a circle that begins and ends with God.

Chapter Twelve

LETTING GO
WITH GRACE

Agape Oil

4 ounces olive oil
12 drops myrrh essential oil
12 drops frankincense essential oil
8 drops sandalwood essential oil
8 drops lavender essential oil

Pour all of the ingredients into a glass
container and stir to combine. Use this oil to
help someone transition from death to new
life. A descendant of the oils carried to the
tomb by Mary, this oil allows us to grieve a
life and offer love faithfully. With these oils
and with prayers of love, the body can return
to ashes without embalming. The oil empowers
you to let go with grace. This blend of oils

can be used by the bedside when someone
dies, rubbing it on hands, feet, and forehead.

THE FAIRS THAT CAME to town when I was a child dance
in my memory like carousels. I remember looking for my
mom from the painted horse of a carousel and waving at
the first sight of her smiling face.

A few years ago, I took my children to a county fair near
Nashville. The young tightrope walker wore a homemade
glittered vest similar to the skating skirt my mom sewed
for me in the second grade. Music played as he hoisted
himself just a few feet above the ground onto the thin wire.
Behind him a homemade red velvet curtain was closed to
try to cover the trailer where he placed the speakers. We
watched him stroll gracefully back and forth, calling out his
next move as music rang out from the speakers. He drew
us into his world, and for a few minutes he captured our
hearts and minds. Like a snake oil salesman, he performed
a miracle before our eyes as he spun and flipped on the
rope. Sweat poured from his forehead as he made amazing
leaps. He earned every coin and dollar we threw into his
hat. I want to be a snake oil salesman like him, welcoming
people into a magical space and offering them hope. Like
him, I don't need a net, since one can't fall from grace.

Snake oil sellers are like tightrope walkers. Both are itin-
erant in nature. Old faith healers, snake oil salesmen, and

carnival acts tell their stories to willing crowds who want to be moved. This road contains a few bumps and potholes that remind us that we're sojourners in this world. While foxes have holes and birds have nests, we don't always have a place to lay our heads. Our journey includes side roads and sideshows; our calling is healing the hurting along the path. The roads to Mecca, Jerusalem, and the Bodhi tree are the sacred path. The people and events we encounter prepare our hearts for the destination.

I live less than five miles from the house I grew up in. I have traveled for years, and I always return home. Even when I am traveling as a snake oil seller, I carry with me the stories of my youth, my family, old healers, all the women who have graced the threshold of Magdalene, and my deep desire to find communion with God. A central place on the journey for me is the communion table at the A-frame chapel built in the 1950s where I serve as priest. This holy place is a home where I can become centered before I head out again. I don't have to buy or sell anything but can stand in a circle and feast on love before heading back out to heal and serve. All healers need such a place.

I've stood at the same altar for almost twenty years. I recently served communion to a woman with a blister on the inside of her thumb. Such a blister is synonymous with yard work—the emblem of a long day's pruning bushes, cutting weeds, pushing a mower, and raking.

The woman's husband, a beautiful man who built a house out in the country, died earlier in the year. He loved their big yard and spent his free time mowing and caring for the land. The blister brought an image to my mind of her standing outside the house alone, tackling some overgrown weeds, and feeling the sting of widowhood in her eyes from sweat and memories. I longed to bend down and kiss the blister, feeling the pain of what she has endured. The blister was sacramental, an outward and visible sign of an inward and spiritual journey that she has walked through.

She reminded me of my mother, who, after working sixty hours during the week, would get up at six o'clock in the morning on Saturdays to get to the grocery store early. Then she would start to mow the lawn just as Nashville temperatures climbed into the nineties. The whole endeavor was exacerbated by the fact that she had a terrible lawnmower. I remember watching her yank on the cord to start the mower, the engine refusing to ignite. She worked up a sweat before the first blade of grass was cut.

I hated that all the neighbors could see her struggle to start the mower. I hated that they couldn't see how graceful she was handling everything and all of us by herself. I hated that we didn't have enough money to buy a better mower, and I really hated that her husband had died and left her with the damn grass to cut.

When I saw the woman's hand at the communion rail, I knew that the blister would heal and that the sting of being a new widow would fade, but for that moment in the circle, the blister stood as a symbol that life is tender and everything we know passes, and that all we have is this sweet moment in a circle full of love. I pressed a bite of bread into her open palm, feeling nothing but love for her. I wasn't giving her the body of Christ as much she embodied the body of Christ. The marks on her hands proved she loved another soul. She was a vision to behold, because she had let go of what she loved the most. She was walking the path alone with grace.

Sometimes letting go is hard, not because we will lose something or someone we love, but because the process of releasing requires us to contemplate our own shortcomings and fears. The work of Magdalene has taught me—slowly—that we can never hold on to the women who cross our threshold and enter the program. At times, I'm tempted to think, *Oh my! We have invested hundreds of hours, thousands of dollars, our hearts and reputation, and now this beautiful woman has returned to the streets.* Sometimes I begin questioning if the healing and work is real.

Several women in the community of Magdalene died from relapsing years after completing the program. Rosalyn, a graduate of the program, was beaten to death, her body found on the Fourth of July. The newspaper didn't seem to mention her death or the fact that at first they couldn't identify the body.

Rosalyn overcame huge obstacles to reclaim her life and become independent. A quiet learner, she dedicated herself to prayer. Two years after she got clean from living on streets and in jail, I went to her to bless her home. She was so proud of her accomplishments. At the time, she was unwavering in her desire to stay clean and sober, but after her graduation from Magdalene she made some bad decisions. In the final year of her life, she was in an abusive relationship, suffered a relapse, and lost her job, home, and car before being murdered.

At the news of her death, I grieved for more than Rosalyn. I mourned for all women still suffering on streets, vulnerable to being beaten beyond recognition and dying. I wept in the face of the truth that we can't hold on to people. I grieved that loneliness is some of the worst pain we can know, which makes you never want to let go of someone or even never love them in the first place. If we let ourselves grieve for one woman killed, our hearts may break under the heaviness of senseless violence and private suffering throughout the world. Grieving all the women throughout the United States, Rwanda, Ecuador, and across the world who suffer rape and murder is a weight that seems impossible to handle. But if we allow ourselves the privilege of mourning all suffering, our grief instead strengthens us to powerfully love and diligently work in our efforts to heal.

My heart goes out to Rosalyn's family and to all her sisters in Magdalene who loved her. I mourned her with fond memories. As a community, we celebrated the years she embraced a sober life. We remembered her by name at the communion table in the chapel.

Rosalyn knew violence most of her life and still tried to find love and acceptance. Her life teaches me that it is right to be concerned about all the women in this world who are walking the streets. We can't rest on our good deeds or sweet prayers. We have to keep working and be dogged in our desire to see healing in this world. We have to continue to leave the safety of communion rails and speak truth in alleys and prisons—anywhere people will listen.

Watching a precious life slip through your fingers because of death or relapse is painful. Sometimes the only way to bear it is to count the last days in hours. Sometimes I wonder how I will get through the next hour of the work at Magdalene, or the next hour of being a mom, or the next hour of serving as a pastor. Hours don't pass evenly like the rhythm of chimes on a grandfather clock. They speed by and then slam to a halt. Some stretch out long enough to wrap around our hearts and live in a memory of the past. Others whiz by before we can catch sight of them. To me, an hour is like a long short story.

Beginning in the last part of the twelfth chapter of John, Jesus says that his hour has come as he begins saying goodbye to his disciples. Many hours have passed since the beginning of John's Gospel, when Jesus talks about God loving the whole world.[1] Hours have passed since Jesus healed, retreated, and grieved his friend Lazarus. Hours have passed since a woman anointed Jesus lavishly for burial. When Jesus says the hour has come, he means that of all the hours of his life, the one marking his death has come. This is the climax and the culmination of love. He tries to explain that a grain of wheat must fall to produce a greater yield. The imagery is one of death in order to produce life. In this hour, what we have lived for becomes how we are remembered. The passage becomes the prelude to Jesus' farewell discourse, in which he says no greater love exists than laying down your life for a friend.[2] We are called to live for love and pray we die glorifying love.

Millions of hours have passed since Jesus spoke those words before his death, but the truth has not changed. To live and die for love is the essence of discipleship. Death is the hour that seals our life and that we fear and face. Jesus teaches us that even in that hour love can be glorified. Our prayer is that in letting go in death, our healing continues into the other side of time. The prayer is that we can explode in an "Alleluia!" even as we make the grave our bed. To get there we have to walk through this hour, not just in scripture but also in our lives. When we accept this hour, we live and die to glorify love.

Death is the hour we walk closest to our creator and hold on to the truth. The power of this hour eclipses all the other hours. The hour of our death is akin to the hour we sit through during labor as we count breaths and watch and wait and pray. It is the hour we anticipate and fear in the middle of the night when shadows seem real and prayers feel hollow—it's as hard and disillusioning as witnessing love hanging from the crucifixes of our lives. I have witnessed folks glorify love in this hour. People will weep for the kindness of strangers and tenderness they have known. People who are lying in hospice thank every single person who walks through the door. People remember only what they love as they say goodbye.

A man named Reid had recently started coming to services at the chapel. He came a few months ago for a weekday service and the next day his aorta exploded. He endured a fifteen-hour surgery and a horrible infection that placed him on death's doorstep in the ICU. A week later, still in ICU, his eyes were filled with love that poured out in sweet streams on his cheeks. He said, "They thought I would die. I thought I would die. But this morning, lying here, watching the rain hit the window, I realized it doesn't get any better than this. I know that sounds crazy, and maybe I should want other things, but truly, I feel like listening to this rain, at this moment, life doesn't get better."

The man broke the hourglass and lived in an eternal moment where he saw time was filled with grains of sand that taken alone were enough to contemplate the wonder of the universe itself. When I visited him in his hour, he wasn't thinking of regrets or mourning; he had already let all of that go. He was filled with gratitude for the eternal present moment he was experiencing.

When my hour comes, I hope the communities I serve will want to continue to visit the people labeled as forsaken or, at least, forgotten on the side roads of the world. The biggest gift of my life is traveling in those circles. I believe that when we let go of all the places and times we have allowed injustices and pain to wash over us, and we let go of everything else, we are left with the energy to act on our desire to help soothe the suffering and mend our hearts. When we can let go and find the freedom to wander again, we get to experience the truth that love is enough. God fills the spaces where there is nothing else. When I die, I will be healed. When you die, you will be healed. Before then, we will keep offering balms and oils, keep holding one another, and keep praying for grace.

In Genesis, when Joseph brings his father, Jacob, to Pharaoh during their sojourn into Egypt during a famine, Jacob says that he has been making this pilgrimage for more than a hundred years. He says those hundred years are nothing in comparison to how long his forefathers wandered.[3] Jacob and Joseph teach us what they learned during their wandering: everything we have comes from God, so we give back to God and our neighbors only what came from God's generosity in the first place. This is a great image of the gifts of creation being passed back and forth and all around. We receive the gifts from creation in oils and offer them lavishly to one another, knowing they were never ours to begin with. They were just passing through our grateful hands.

I once dreamed about letting go. I dreamed I was invited to speak in a grand cathedral with castle turrets and marbled spires. The church looked just like the place in Oz where the wizard lived. I stood in the back of this huge palace, practicing the sermon I was preparing, ready to preach about the story of Moses on Mount Sinai. In my dream, I watched as Moses ascended the mountain after leading the people in exodus and through the desert. I listened as God agreed to show Moses the back of his head, and I saw Moses hide in the cleft of a rock near a precipice as God's glory passes by. The story turns in my dream, however. As

God passes by Moses, he whispers, "Fly." Moses picks up a stick, then stands and leans over the cliff, and throws the stick to see how far it falls.

Just as I was about to finish practicing my sermon, I heard people from the front of the church announce the Gospel. I had to start running down the long aisle to the front of the cathedral and the grandest pulpit I had ever seen. I ran on marble, and then realized I was running on broken stones, and then I ran in a long field with a stone path that continued forever. There was no grand cathedral or pulpit. I was just running forever. I woke up exhausted and wondered, *When is it enough?*

Doesn't it seem like Moses did enough? He served God for more than a hundred years, endured the murmuring of the people, led them for forty years, and God still wanted him to fly? Of course, God never told Moses to fly—this was just my dream. Instead God kept Moses close, and when God told Moses it was time for him to lie down to die, Moses sang a song of gratitude for the gift of serving. That is the quintessential example of faithfulness. Out in the field with no grand cathedrals we are reminded to sing in gratitude for any service we have been able to offer.

In the real life of faith, "When is it enough?" is not a question. The life of faith calls us to continually serve on the path of love. When we get that straight in our minds, we remember there's always enough. We're not going to run out of ways to serve or the means by which we can serve. If we're still asking, "Is that enough?" we aren't on the right path. In the Gospels, Jesus dispels all the worries about enough by reminding the disciples that a mustard seed is more than enough.

Snake oil salesmen will always be with us; this is a blessing, not a curse. Whether they come in Wild West shows or as Appalachian healers, witch doctors, aroma therapists, priests, infomercial hawkers, or faith healers, they will always come, as long as people are willing to listen to a good story. We can choose to appreciate the story and never forget our roots—like the roots of a bloodroot plant, which bleed a bright orange and can heal our kidneys, or like the roots that carry us back to the ancient trees that once anointed kings and were seen as a gift of God, or like the roots that belong to the trees of visions that clap their hands in joy and weep by the river of our pain. True snake oil sellers beckon, "Come unto me all of you that labor and I will ease your pain." They invite us like the eternal sky to keep searching for truth and meaning.

I stumbled into this vocation and now embrace the work fully. I hope more people will join me as sellers of healing snake oil. We need more good old-fashioned healers with fine oils. We need oils whose liquid gold illuminates dark spaces and whose fragrance can fill any void. Oils will carry us around the world and help us set deep roots into this very earth that holds us up every day. Oils allow us to dig into the earth and find the gifts of creation given to us by a loving creator. The oils carry us back to our cousins, the prophets.

I am a snake oil seller, and I am selling a movement along with a product. I am selling a movement that refuses to accept a culture that buys and sells other human beings. I am selling a movement that believes that violence against women and trauma do not get the last word—love does. I am selling a movement of thousands and thousands of women who believe in freedom and economic justice for all women. I am selling a movement that demystifies prostitution and trafficking so we can have honest conversations about why women walk the streets and what it means to welcome them home. I am selling a movement that does not accept the argument that because prostitution is the oldest form of sexual abuse, we cannot change its wake of violence and addiction. I am selling a movement that believes love is the strongest force for social change that we have.

I will keep going to the sanctuary and the marketplace, calling for a more just world and selling the healing balm of Gilead.

About the Author

BECCA STEVENS is an Episcopal priest, social entrepreneur, snake oil salesman, thistle farmer, speaker, and author of five books. For Becca, ministry and writing are practical endeavors. She is chaplain of St. Augustine's at Vanderbilt University. She is also founder and executive director of Magdalene, a residential community for women who have survived lives of trafficking, violence, prostitution, and addiction, as well as its social enterprise, Thistle Farms. Becca maintains a commitment to the truth that love is the most powerful force for change in the world.

Becca has raised almost $15 million in private and corporate gifts and gained nationwide press coverage for her work. She has won awards from the Frist Foundation and the Academy for Women of Achievement. Named "Alumnus of the Year" by the University of the South and "Nashvillian of the Year" by the *Nashville Scene*, Becca was selected as "Tennessean of the Year" by *The Tennessean*. In 2011 the White House named her one of fifteen Champions of Change for women who have known abuse and sexual violence.

She has been featured on NPR, the PBS series *Turning Point*, and Fox News. In addition to having written numerous articles, Becca is a widely traveled speaker and has both a blog and podcasts available online at www .beccastevens.org. Becca lives in Nashville with her husband, Grammy-winning songwriter Marcus Hummon, and their three sons, Levi, Caney, and Moses.

About Magdalene and Thistle Farms

Thistle Farms healing oils in the thistle box.

THISTLE FARMS IS A social enterprise for women who have survived lives of prostitution, trafficking, addiction, and life on the streets. By hand, the women create natural body care products that are as kind to the earth as they are to the body. All sales proceeds go back into Thistle Farms and the two-year residential communities, Magdalene. Residents receive housing, food, medical and dental expenses, therapy, education, and job training—all at no cost to them. Magdalene and Thistle Farms take no government funding but rely solely on gifts from individuals and organizations and the sale of Thistle Farms products. Magdalene and Thistle Farms stand as a witness to the truth that in the end, love is most powerful force for change in the world.

The Symbol of the Thistle

Considered a weed, thistles grow on the streets and in the alleys where the women of Magdalene and Thistle Farms have walked. But thistles have a deep taproot that grows through thick concrete and survives drought. And in spite of their prickly appearance, their soft purple center makes thistles mysterious and gorgeous flowers. Being a thistle farmer means the world is our farm. Harvesting thistles is a way of walking in the world and choosing to love the parts of creation that others have forgotten or condemned.

Notes

Chapter Four

1 A recipe for mock apple pie
  (a kind of snake oil for sure)
  2 cups water
  1 cup white sugar
  2 teaspoons cream of tartar
  30 buttery round crackers
  1 recipe pastry for a 9-inch single-crust pie
  1 teaspoon ground cinnamon
  1 tablespoon lemon juice
  1 cup crushed buttery round crackers
  ½ cup packed brown sugar
  ⅓ cup butter, melted

  Preheat oven to 425°F (220°C).
  In a saucepan over medium high heat, combine
      the water, sugar, and cream of tartar; bring
      to boil.
  Drop in whole crackers and boil for 5 minutes.
      Pour mixture into pie shell; sprinkle with
      ½ teaspoon cinnamon and lemon juice.

Mix together the crushed crackers, brown sugar, remaining cinnamon, and butter; sprinkle over pie filling.

Bake for 15 minutes and reduce heat to 375°F (190°C) and continue to bake for 15 to 20 minutes longer. Serve warm.

Chapter Five

1 Psalm 60:7.
2 Exodus 30:23–35.

Chapter Seven

1 Isaiah 6:8.
2 As quoted from the Book of Common Prayer, p. 833.

Chapter Eight

1 Ezekiel 16:6–7.
2 Amos 5:24.

Chapter Nine

1 John 12:8.
2 http://www.sharedhope.org/Portals/0/Documents /SHI_National_Report_on_DMST_2009%28without _cover%29.pdf.
3 Deuteronomy 34:4–5.

Chapter Eleven

1 Book of Common Prayer, Prayers to use at the time of death, p. 521.

2 You can learn more about this book on our website at
   www.thistlefarms.org.

Chapter Twelve

1 John 3:16.
2 John 15:13.
3 Genesis 47:9.